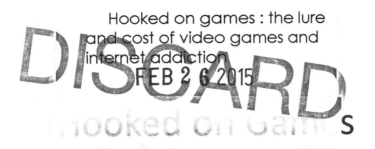

Hooked on Games

*The Lure and Cost of Video Game
and Internet Addiction*

Andrew Doan, MD, PhD with Brooke Strickland

Foreword by Douglas Gentile, PhD

The views expressed in this book are those of the author and do not
necessarily reflect the official policy or position of the Department of
the Navy, Department of Defense, or the United States Government.
All the stories of video game addiction and excessive play are true. Most
of the names of people discussed in this book have been changed to
protect their identities and privacy. Descriptions of video game play and
scenarios are based on real video games from the authors' experiences.
NO MEDICAL ADVICE IS GIVEN NOR IS ANY PROVIDED IN THIS BOOK. SUCH
INFORMATION WHICH MAY BE MEDICAL IN NATURE IS INFORMATION ONLY
FOR THE USE OF LICENSED AND EXPERIENCED MEDICAL PRACTITIONERS.
A READER INTERESTED IN MEDICAL ADVICE OR TREATMENT SHOULD
CONSULT A MEDICAL PRACTITIONER WITH AN APPROPRIATE SPECIALTY
WHO IS PROPERLY LICENSED IN THE READER'S JURISDICTION.

Copyright © 2012 Andrew Doan, MD, PhD,
and Brooke Strickland

Hooked on Games: The Lure and Cost of
Video Game and Internet Addiction

By Andrew Doan, MD, PhD with Brooke Strickland

Foreword by Douglas Gentile, PhD

Edited by Louise Damberg and Marie Hunt

Published and distributed by F.E.P. International, Inc.

www.fepint.org

www.hooked-on-games.com

PRINTED IN THE UNITED STATES OF AMERICA

FOR INFORMATION WRITE F.E.P. INTERNATIONAL, INC.

941 25TH AVENUE, #101 CORALVILLE, IA 52241

ISBN 978-1-935576-02-0

TYPESETTING AND COVER DESIGN BY DANIEL HUNT

I appreciate you taking the time to read my story. If you find my book helpful, please pass it on to someone else who may benefit from my message. Please support my mission in educating the world about the lure and dangers of video game and Internet addiction by sharing my book on Facebook, Twitter, and providing a book review on Amazon.com and other online retailers.

Andrew Doan, MD, PhD

www.andrew-doan.com
www.hooked-on-games.com

ACKNOWLEDGEMENTS

I thank my gorgeous wife, Julie, who demonstrated the patience of Job and prayed for me when all hope appeared lost. I thank my church home, Celebrate Recovery, and the Men's Group at Rancho Community Church for their friendships and guidance. Special thanks goes out to Jesus Christ, my Lord and Savior. Without God's intervention and love, I would not be here today to share my story.

Table of Contents

Table of Contents

Foreword

People have been talking about video games and the Internet being "addictive" ever since games and computers entered the home. As a gamer and Internet user, I recognize the temptation to call them addictive, but, as a scientist, I am deeply skeptical. Although we use the term "addiction" colloquially in the culture to describe anything with which we spend a lot of time, this is not the proper way to describe video gaming, either medically or psychologically.

Addictions (and indeed, most mental health disorders) are defined by how much they disrupt one's life, not by how much it is used. Moreover, to be classified as clinically significant, it requires dysfunction in multiple areas of life. Because time is limited, we always sacrifice some activities for others that we prefer. Therefore, if you love gaming and give up some time with your family to game, that alone does not indicate an addiction. In fact, that makes it normal. But if your family and friendships are suffering, you are doing poorly in school, or your work life is suffering, then the gaming has caused you to be dysfunctional because it is clearly related to damaging multiple important areas of your life.

I began studying video game addiction using this much more conservative clinical approach to define the issue. I was a true scientific skeptic, and I honestly believed that I would not find any people who fit this more clinical definition of addiction. But the data do not lie, and it turned out that a surprising number of gamers admitted damage to multiple areas of their lives. In one national study of over 1,100 8 to 18-year-olds in the United States, we found that 8.5 percent would classify as pathological gamers by this definition. Although this could be considered a somewhat small percentage, the true nature of the problem becomes clear when one considers this percentage in population terms. There are about forty million children between eight and eighteen in the United States. Approximately 90 percent of them play video games. If 8.5 percent of them are pathological, that's over 3 million children seriously damaging multiple areas of their lives because of their gaming habits! That's over 3 million children who probably should get some help, but most won't because there is no medical diagnosis for the pathological use of technology. Once there is, it will be similar to the approach focusing on dysfunction. The medical diagnostic definition matters because, until there is one, insurance companies will not pay for treatment.

In addition, many therapists are not yet convinced that it is a "real" problem. This is similar to where we were with alcoholism fifty years ago. Studies were beginning to come out suggesting that it looked like a medical disease model would fit; there were identifiable risk factors, and it could be treated, but most people did not simply get better without help. The culture, however, was not able to accept this at the time. Instead, the culture considered it to be a moral failing—alcoholics just weren't "strong enough." It took thirty years of research to demonstrate that alcoholism should be taken seriously by the medical community. I believe we are at a similar point with the pathological use of technology.

Studies are beginning to show that it looks like there are identifiable risk factors; for example, it does not go away on its own easily, and it can be treated. In one study of over 3,000 children, the researchers found that they could predict which children would become pathological gamers by knowing if they had poor impulse control, poor social relationships, and spent a lot of time gaming *(Choo H, Gentile DA, Sim T, Li D, Khoo A, Liau AK. Pathological video-gaming among Singaporean youth. Ann Acad Med Singapore. 2010 Nov;39(11):822-9; Gentile DA, Choo H, Liau A, Sim T, Li D, Fung D, Khoo A. Pathological video game use among youths: a two-year longitudinal study. Pediatrics. 2011 Feb;127(2):e319-29. Epub 2011 Jan 17).*

Once they became pathological gamers, they became more depressed, anxious, socially phobic, and less productive in school. If they stopped being addicted, their depression, anxiety, and social phobias lifted, and their grades improved. It appeared that the gaming was an important part of their overall mental health.

Yet, the broader culture is still resistant to this message, and they consider gaming addiction to be a moral failing; only this time, the moral failing is usually assumed to be that of the parents, who are expected to be able to control the behavior of their children. Certainly more research is needed before the medical community feels that we understand the problem enough to come to an agreed-upon definition. Nonetheless, I hope it does not take another thirty years of research before we begin to take this issue seriously.

Douglas A. Gentile, PhD
www.douglasgentile.com

Introduction: Hooked on Games

Shawn Woolley had many friends and an active social life. You'd often find Shawn trying to make people laugh. He enjoyed interacting with people, and he grew up as a happy and well-adjusted child. As he approached early adulthood, he purchased a car, moved out into his own apartment, and was promoted to assistant manager at his workplace.

But something quickly changed. Shawn discovered and began to engross himself in the fantasy world of the role-playing video game *EverQuest*. According to his mother, Liz, his personality started changing because of his devotion to and significant obsession with the game. He started playing for hours on end, and some nights, he wouldn't sleep; he would literally stay up all night, immersing himself in the world of *EverQuest*. Fully absorbed in this game, Shawn's personal life began to deteriorate. He lost friendships, his job, his car, and his apartment. He eventually lost his Internet connection—his tie to the fantasy world. Without access to the Internet, Shawn became desperate.

Late one night, Shawn's mother heard a noise in the main floor of her home. She thought it was an intruder, but when she descended the stairs she was shocked to find Shawn sitting in front of her computer, playing *Ever-Quest*. He had walked four miles during the night and broken into his mother's home in order to get access to the game.

Shawn's mother acquired help from clinical therapists and doctors, all of whom did not understand video game addiction. They said that she should be glad he wasn't addicted to something more severe, like drugs or alcohol. Shawn took this as a green light to keep playing. He dove more deeply into the world of *EverQuest*, neglecting everything that had once been important to him. The line between the real world and the virtual world blurred. In the precious few moments he was not immersed in the game, he suffered hallucinations as images from his fantasy game world bled into reality.

But one day, something troubling happened in the game. He had created a character called ILUVYOU. His mother believes that he had developed a relationship with another gamer, and he used his ILUVYOU character to court her. He was so attached and committed to this relationship that when something the other player said hurt him, Shawn stopped playing on the same server. He left all of his online friends and isolated himself from his real-life family and friends. He did not take care of himself and lost interest in everything. He no longer resembled the social, fun man he used to be. Three weeks later, Shawn sat down in front of the computer, and while the game was idle on the screen, he put a loaded gun to his head. Shawn was isolated from his family and friends, not only in real life, but also in the fantasy world of *EverQuest*. He was totally alone. He fired a single shot. Shawn Woolley was dead at twenty-one years old.[1]

Why would someone commit suicide over a video game? How could a young man who once had everything going for him give himself up so completely to a game that he ultimately pulled a trigger to end his life?

Many video games like *EverQuest* are extremely addictive. Also referred to as *EverCrack* by gamers, *EverQuest* is known to have great addictive potential. Increasing demand for video games and growing revenues drive the video game companies to create fun, engaging, and addictive games. A successful game may generate billions of dollars in revenue by attracting and retaining devoted players. Successful video games are designed to be engaging and enticing and, therefore, can be extremely addictive.

A study completed by Dr. Douglas Gentile at Iowa State University looked at 1,178 cross-sectional children and

---

1 KOHN, DAVID. "ADDICTED: SUICIDE OVER EVERQUEST?" CBS NEWS. FEBRUARY 11, 2009. HTTP://WWW.CBSNEWS.COM/ STORIES/2002/10/17/48HOURS/MAIN525965.SHTML. ACCESSED SEPTEMBER 13, 2011.

teens (aged eight to eighteen) across America. The study showed that 88 percent of the kids surveyed played video games. Video games are widely accessible and present in almost every American home. The results of the Iowa State University study indicated that 8.5 percent of the children who played video games showed signs of addiction to gaming, similar to addictive gambling behavior.[2] Based on recent census data and the addiction rate reported by the Iowa State University study, there are likely at least 3 million kids addicted to video games in the United States. There are now four decades of video gamers, and there may be as many as 12 million Americans addicted to video games. Worldwide, the addiction rate seems to be similar, according to Dr. Gentile.

An Associated Press–AOL Games poll showed that 40 percent of American adults played either online or console video games.[3] As video games become more intricate and the video graphics become more lifelike (which I refer to as digital eye candy) the games become increasingly enticing. The realistic graphics and gameplay contribute to the immersion of the player into a digital world. The digital worlds these video games provide are pleasing, challenging, and can be more fun than the real world.

---

2 GENTILE, DOUGLAS. "PATHOLOGICAL VIDEO-GAME USE AMONG YOUTH AGES 8 TO 18." PSYCHOL SCI. 2009 JUN; 20(6):785.
3 "SURVEY: FOUR IN 10 AMERICAN ADULTS PLAY VIDEO GAMES." FOXNEWS.COM. MAY 9, 2006. HTTP://WWW.FOXNEWS.COM/STORY/0,2933,194659,00.HTML. ACCESSED JULY 15, 2011.

Video games are also more popular and generate more business than movies and many other forms of entertainment. In a report published by *Newzoo*, consumer spending reached nearly $25 billion annually for games in 2010; this included mobile device games, casual game portals, social networking games, consoles, and both boxed and downloadable computer games.[4] The video game industry has become a multi-billion dollar industry.

One of my good friends, Charles Wahlheim, is an actor and model. He was hired to perform a fighting scene for a video game. When he arrived on the set, he was amazed that the producers had rented a green screen nearly seventy-five yards long. Previously, Charles had been on big movie sets that didn't have nearly as large of a green screen. For a video game, the enormous green screen was impressive. The set was packed with nearly a hundred people. He inquired about the budget for the video game and was shocked to learn that it was nearly $100 million, equivalent to the money budgeted for major motion pictures.

Clearly, not all people who play video games become addicted. Video games are not evil; they are part of our culture and are here to stay. They are a fun form of en-

4 BARLEY, MARK. "CONSUMER SPENDING ON VIDEO GAMES REACHES $25 BILLION." HOOKED! GAMERS. DECEMBER 22, 2010. WEB. JULY 16, 2011. HTTP://WWW.HOOKEDGAMERS.COM/BLOGS/MARKBARLEY/2010/12/22/CONSUMER_SPENDING_ON_VIDEO_GAMES_REACHES_25_BILLION.HTM. ACCESSED JULY 15, 2011.

tertainment and a source of education when used responsibly and in moderation. There are people who drink alcohol who do not become alcoholics. There are people who gamble who do not become addicted gamblers. The issue is lack of widespread public education about the potential dangers of excessive video game playing.

While parents do not generally provide access to alcohol, cigarettes, and gambling for their children, video games are widely accepted as safe, healthy entertainment for children in nearly all homes. There is growing evidence in the medical literature documenting the severe emotional and physical consequences of excessive video game playing and video game addiction. There are numerous news stories of severe neglect, poor health, and even death associated with excessive playing of video games.

Parents, spouses, and families of gamers often ask me why video games are addictive, seeking to discover insight into why a loved one is mesmerized by the digital world. This book will show you how and why people are addicted to video games and why games are inherently enticing and potentially addictive. The addiction is associated with behavioral rewards and neurochemical changes in the human brain. We also reveal the health risks that stem from video game addiction. This book provides insight into my obsession and addiction to video games, the steps for recovery, and advice for families and friends of video game addicts.

As a physician with both a medical degree and a doctoral degree in neuroscience from The Johns Hopkins University, School of Medicine, I have researched medical and scientific literature as well as news articles on how gaming can rewire the brain. Video game addiction is similar to other behavioral addictions such as food, shopping, sex, and gambling addiction. Video game addiction can even be as powerful and destructive as severe drug and alcohol abuse. Most importantly, I have experienced first-hand the adverse effects of video game addiction. A former game addict, I played more than 20,000 hours of video games over a period of 9 years. I will share how I almost lost everything important to me due to gaming addiction—my family, a prestigious medical career, and even my life.

Chapter 1: Escape From Reality

It was the spring of 1975 and I had just turned four years old. My country had been at war fighting a communist government for nearly two decades. I was part of a wealthy family living in South Vietnam. My mother was an entrepreneur and my father served as an officer in the South Vietnamese Army. Both my parents were well connected in the community. That spring, rumors were circulating that we were going to lose Saigon and that the United States military was leaving. My parents, who feared the worst, stashed away diamonds and other valuable heirlooms in preparation for leaving the country.

My parents were not only afraid, but, as successful business owners, they were saddened to have to abandon over two-dozen workers employed at their clothing business. It also saddened them to leave my grandparents behind. My maternal grandfather couldn't find my grandmother the day we left Saigon, and so he refused to abandon his wife and stayed behind to find her. My uncle, an officer in the South Vietnamese Army, knew about a Taiwanese ship evacuating people to the Philippines. Our family was instructed to meet at a hangar located on the military base. Space was limited. My parents paid bribes to have our entire family—aunts, uncles, and cousins—evacuated. Our family of seven hid in a dark, crowded hangar with hundreds of other men and women, where we knew we would be safe. The next morning, everyone was evacuated. That same day, Saigon fell.

After being evacuated to the Philippines, my family was transported to Wake Island, a small coral atoll in the North Pacific Ocean with a coastline of only twelve miles. I came down with chickenpox, and the whole family was quarantined for a month so I could recover from the illness. My sister recalled the absence of air conditioning in the barracks and the hot, humid summer on Wake Island. Upon being released, my family was relocated to "Tent City".

Tent City was a temporary facility erected at Camp Pendleton in Southern California to house that first influx of 50,000 Vietnamese refugees in the United States after the fall of Saigon. After I had recovered, my parents decided it was time to move on. They wanted their children to adapt to American life, integrate into American culture. They insisted we learn English, make friends, and adopt a completely different lifestyle in this new country. Instead of staying in Southern California where there were literally thousands of other Vietnamese families, my parents decided to move the family to Aberdeen, South Dakota where there were very few other Vietnamese families. My parents believed that by separation from Vietnamese communities and immersion into American communities, their children would learn English more quickly and have greater opportunities. This strategy worked. I have no discernable Vietnamese accent, though English was not my first language and Vietnamese was spoken exclusively within my home while I was growing up. With the help of a supportive church that embraced our family, we were able to move into a house, and my father was able to find work as a janitor and as a musical instrument repairman.

Our first winter in South Dakota was miserable. As a four-year-old child used to tropical weather and humidity, my first winter in the United States was a shock. I was not accustomed to the sub-zero temperatures of the Midwest. My parents didn't know how to turn on the heat, so they burned charcoal in the house to keep warm, eventually poisoning the entire family with carbon monoxide gas. This resulted in our being treated at the local emergency room.

As time passed we continued to find it very difficult to adapt to the frigid temperatures in South Dakota. When I was about six, my parents decided to pack up once again and move the family closer to the West Coast. The gold and jewelry that my parents had brought with them to America was worth a significant amount of money, and my parents launched something unheard of in 1970s Portland, Oregon, a Vietnamese grocery store and restaurant.

I still have fond memories of being in my parents' grocery store. I had access to a seemingly unlimited supply of candy bars. One of my sisters wanted a charm bracelet being offered by Nestle Crunch. In order to receive the charm bracelet, we had to mail in numerous candy bar wrappers. I was recruited to eat an entire box of Crunch bars. To date, I cannot bear eating a single one.

My family was living the American dream. We owned a home and had started a business; but for me, the dream began turning into a nightmare. When I was seven, I occasionally "manned" the cash register for a brief time when my sisters were busy helping my parents. At the cash register, I made paper guns and gun holsters. I wanted to be the Lone Ranger, and I admired John Wayne. One evening, I was recovering from an ear infection and sat at the register, busily day-dreaming about being a Western hero. A couple of young men walked into the store and, seeing a young boy at the cash register, stole a case of beer and ran. As a kid who desperately wanted to embrace the American lifestyle and embody what it meant to be a Western hero, I chased after them, to no avail. I returned to my parents' store, defeated. I was punished with a slap in the face by one of my sisters for not alarming the family that customers had walked into the store. Because of the ear infection, the pain was excruciating. It was a sharp reminder that my daydreams were only that, dreams; I was not a Western hero, but just a kid from an immigrant family. That slap still resonates with me today.

I had no Asian role models. I had no Vietnamese friends. My family was struggling, feeling the pressures of trying to adjust to life in a completely new world. As a young boy, I absorbed this stress. The restaurant and grocery business eventually failed; it was one of many failed businesses because my parents knew little English and did not understand American business practices. Eventually, my family lost all of the wealth that they had brought with them from Vietnam. Living in America was painfully difficult, and my parents never seemed happy.

To support a family with four kids, my mother, father, and aunt all found jobs at a growing company in Beaverton, Oregon called Tektronix. Tektronix manufactured electronic testing equipment, printers, and circuit boards for electronic devices. Because my aunt and mother did not speak English well, they worked as assembly line workers, making minimum wage. My dad, who knew more English, became an electronic technician.

Growing up in a nearly all-Caucasian, blue-collar community, I found it difficult to fit in with the typical American boys. For one, I did not look like the other American kids. I had squinty brown eyes, and the other kids' eyes seemed to be all beautiful shades of blue. I was dark, and my skin looked dirty to me compared to the other kids' skin, which seemed clean and white. I had a funny Vietnamese name, Phuong Duc Doan, and the other kids had really cool-sounding names like Brian, Mike and Larry. My family was poor, and during the winter there was frost on the windows inside the house because my parents turned down the heat to save money. The other kids seemed to have so much wealth with all their fancy toys and warm homes.

For these reasons, I was the perfect candidate for video game addiction. It was easy for me to turn to video games to block out what was going on around me and to embrace the world that they offered. Video games gave me a way to finally become the hero I had longed to be when I chased after the thieves who robbed my family. I had control in the digital world. I felt safe in the digital world. I felt powerful in the digital world. At the age of nine, I played *Space Invaders* on the Atari 2600 for the first time at a friend's house and became totally enamored with it. I wanted nothing more than to have a console for myself. As the following Christmas approached, that's all I could talk about. Even though I knew money was extremely tight for my family, I begged my parents desperately for an Atari 2600 gaming system.

My parents, who fiercely loved me and wanted to do everything they could to help me become a part of the American culture, sacrificed greatly that year. Even with their low incomes, my parents and aunt saved what money they could to get me an Atari 2600 gaming console and *Space Invaders*, along with several other games for Christmas. I was so obsessed with acquiring the games that I talked about it incessantly. Finally, my father took me to the mall on Christmas Eve. As I walked into the toy store toward the video games, I felt tingles of anticipation throughout my body. I felt euphoric, excited, and anxious to return home to play.

After I first set up my Atari 2600, I remembered completely losing myself in the game of *Space Invaders*. The stress, the fights in the house, the struggles to fit in and become something I wasn't, and the pressure to make a name for myself—all the stressors of my life melted away that night when I played that game. I found peace. I discovered a way to escape. I was able to blast away aliens, much like the thoughts and pressures that invaded my spirit daily. I was able to conquer, and for once I felt in control of my life.

That first day, I played the Atari 2600 for twelve hours

straight. I played so much *Space Invaders* that I went to bed with an excruciating pain in my forearm from hours and hours of pushing a button and moving the joystick back and forth.

As video games evolved, I became more and more absorbed with the digital world. Out in the real world, my life focused on studying hard in school to get good grades so I could become a lawyer or a doctor—to be somebody and live up to my parents' expectations. But when I came home from school, I was a hero saving Princess Toadstool in the digital world of *Super Mario Brothers*. At a young age, I was being trained to push buttons to feel good, like a rat in a Skinner box.

B.F. Skinner, the noted behavioral psychologist, studied operant conditioning while he was a graduate student at Harvard University in the 1930s. He is recognized for his Skinner box experiments, where the subject animal learns by trial and error that pressing a lever yields a reward. When the reward is delivered, the lever-pressing behavior is reinforced. Skinner argued that, with the selection of appropriate rewards, his system of operant conditioning could be used to teach anyone anything. Similar to the behavioral conditioning experiments performed by B.F. Skinner with rats and pigeons, I was being trained to push buttons by playing video games for my digital reward, the digital heroin for my mind. The digital heroin helped me to escape from the reality of being in a poor, immigrant family. Unknowingly, I was reinforcing addictive behaviors with video games as a young child that would later haunt me as an adult.

During my adolescence, I was an easy target for teasing and jokes by all the Caucasian kids at school. I began pursuing sports, particularly baseball. I admired and loved my first baseball coach, Coach Bob. I loved being part of a team and having Coach Bob compliment me on my speed and athletic abilities. He had a powerful impact on my life because he didn't treat me like a Vietnamese immigrant; he treated me like one of his own sons. He treated me like someone who mattered.

Consequently, I loved baseball. At home, I practiced swinging the bat, fielding the ball, and throwing the ball. I worked hours upon hours to master the pop-up slide. With holes in my jeans from practicing so much, I soon became one of the best base runners and players on the team. Other kids on the team, however, bullied and teased me, calling me "Rice Patty." When I assumed my position as shortstop, knees bent, ready to field the ball, I became familiar with taunts and laughter from the Caucasian boys yelling, "Rice patty! Did you eat your rice today, rice picker?!"

Even though I was confident in my abilities in baseball,

the years and years of endless teasing and taunting with spiteful slurs like these chipped away more and more at my already low self-esteem. On top of that, I was mortified when my dad would cheer me on from the stands, banging and clanking pie pans as loudly as he could and yelling out in a thick Asian accent, "You can do it, number one base runner!"

As an adult, I can look back and understand that my dad was extremely proud of me and loved me. However, at the time, my dad yelling on the sidelines were some of the most horrifically embarrassing moments of my life. I became even more insecure, and because of my insecurities, I learned to be a bully to gain more control over my relationships. As a bully, I thought, I was the one who controlled the outcome. I searched for weaknesses in others before they could discover weaknesses in me. I was quick to strike, so that they didn't have the chance to pick on me.

During my ninth grade year in school, I walked the halls with my jock friends, peacocking and strutting to intimidate the other students. One day we encountered a kid in the hallway who was a "Jesus freak." I identified his weaknesses as being overweight and nearsighted, and I picked on him mercilessly for being fat and wearing glasses. Yet, inside, I secretly yearned for the self-confidence that he seemed to possess. My verbal attacks were not affecting him, so I punched him in the chest, unprovoked. He dropped to the ground like a sack of potatoes, started to seize violently, and foamed at the mouth. The ninth grade English teacher, who admired me for my showmanship in the classroom and nearly straight A work ethic, rushed out of her classroom to see me hovering over this kid, nudging his shoulders desperately and asking if he was okay. She asked, "What happened?!" I calmly lied, "I don't know." She trusted my answer and attended to the boy lying on the ground. After minutes, which seemed like hours, he recovered. As a physician, I now realize I could have killed him. He seized because his heart had spasms from the thump on his chest. I could be in prison instead of a physician today if the boy had died.

My solution to fitting in was ultimately making things worse. I felt horrible about what I was doing to people, and so I had added guilt to my already deeply rooted self-loathing. I hated what I was. I hated being Asian. The last thing I wanted was to be was Asian. In reality, I was a Vietnamese immigrant with very low self-esteem. But there was an alternate reality. In the real world, I felt I had nowhere to fit in. But there was another world. Which world would I choose? The one where my parents were always financially burdened, working endlessly to provide, and where people never saw me or accepted me as part of their group? Or would I choose the digital world, where I could save the princess and where I could matter as a person? I made my choice. I indulged in hours upon hours of video games. One hour led to two. Two hours led to four. Four hours led to eight. Every hour of playing contributed to the reinforcement of an addictive behavior associated with video game playing. I stayed away from the traditional addictions of drugs, alcohol, and smoking. Instead I used video games as my digital drug of choice.

In high school, I continued to excel in athletics, lettering in wrestling, baseball, and football. I started dating a girl and simply put gaming on the back burner. When I had free time, however, I played numerous hours of Nintendo and Commodore 64 games. I chose to attend Reed College. I also began research at the Oregon Regional Primate Research Center, where I studied neuroscience, focusing on the study of gene expression in the brain. My new goal and passion in life was medicine. I was driven to help people. During college, I didn't touch video games. Oddly, I didn't have much urge to play video games because I was lifting weights daily, and I was focused on my passion to get into medicine. However, during my first year of medical school after college, my brother-in-law introduced me to the IBM PC 486 computer and the games that were available for it—*Master of Orion, Civilization, Myst, X-COM,* and *Warcraft II The Tides of Darkness*. Unfortunately, these video games were the most addictive elements I had encountered in my life thus far.

Video game addiction sneaks in quickly, and then it owns you. Because it is a relatively new addiction, understanding the root cause of it is key to unveiling the mask that so many children, teenagers, and adults struggle to wear when trying to "feed the beast" of gaming obsession. For many kids, playing video games is a way to escape life in the real world where they are pushed by their parents to excel, demanded by their peers to conform, and pressured on all sides by the expectations of others. Kids have to complete chores and menial tasks, and many of them recognize the need to succeed in school and the demands that come with that. These stresses weigh heavily on growing young people, and as we see today, scores of them are turning to alternative digital worlds to run away from their problems.

But it's not just young people who are struggling with this type of addiction. Adults with relationship problems, bills to pay, conflicts needing resolution, and challenges at work are also dealing with the massive lure of video game addiction. Our society is well known for its ability to provide "quick fixes." Typically, people who play video games are very intelligent and enjoy being challenged. They are enticed into obtaining quick highs in a video game rather than dealing with their life issues. In addition, video games are a preferred choice of entertainment during the economic downturn experienced during the last decade. Because playing video games is relatively inexpensive (especially compared to eating out, going to the movies, or going on a vacation), they provide a cheap entertainment source for individuals to immerse themselves in to escape their troubles.

Unfortunately, video games are also the perfect, albeit harmful, digital pacifiers for children. Place a child in front of an enticing video game, and the child is engaged for hours. Adults who use video games as babysitters may inadvertently be encouraging behavior that can lead to future addiction.

In my situation, my parents encouraged me strongly to stay away from drugs, alcohol, smoking, and gambling—the traditional avenues of addiction. Yet, they gave me unrestricted access to video games. Inevitably, this turned into my vice, my addiction, and a flight from the cruel realities I faced in my daily life. I was the rat in the Skinner box experiment. The lever I pushed was attached to a computer and a screen, and my reward was digital images that provided me with an amazing rush. Video games were the answer I turned to when I needed to fulfill my emotional and spiritual needs as a human being, but they also nearly destroyed everything I loved.

The video game industry as a whole is similar to an enormous digital buffet for the mind. There are games that fit the needs of people everywhere. Whether it's a game where individuals are caretakers or nurturers managing a farm and virtual pets, or where they are warlords or gods conquering enemies and creating new universes, there are games that come in different flavors with different lures that allow virtually anyone to become addicted if they use them enough. Modern society is being lured into the digital world and plugging into it for incredible lengths of time.

Video game addiction involves an escape from reality, no matter the reason. However, to understand why video games are so addictive, it helps to understand the basic human needs that motivate people to seek satisfaction through a virtual source. Such needs include: satisfying curiosity, providing a sense of purpose in life, heightening a sense of invincibility, feeding the ego, offering companionship, satisfying the need for challenges, gratifying the need to be a leader, fulfilling sexual fantasies, and meeting the need for love and acceptance.

Chapter 2: Satisfying Curiosity

In sixth grade, I was selected for the Talented and Gifted Program at my school, where the kids with academic potential were shown how to work with computers. At that time, we had Apple computers on which the teacher taught us basic programming skills. It was exciting. As I sat in front of a beautiful new computer and started learning basic computer language, a new world was opened up to me.

I took this knowledge and asked my parents to get me a Commodore 64, which was very powerful at the time. The Commodore 64 plugged into a conventional TV set and utilized a tape drive for data storage. My parents believed computers were great learning tools, and they purchased an adventure game that required answering math problems to progress through the dungeon. Although I was learning math, and I quickly mastered the problems, I really played to gain new weapons and power to kill the dungeon inhabitants, rats, trolls, and monsters.

I used the Commodore 64 to create games of chance and war games that were based on random number generators and probabilities. Playing video games is similar to gambling. Many video games are based on games of chance and probabilities, where the role of the dice determines death, victory, and reward. The Commodore 64 was extremely powerful, and yet affordable, during its time. I joined and created my own bulletin board systems where gamers dialed in with modems to trade games. At 300 bits per second modem transfer rates, it was excruciatingly painful when someone in my family picked up the phone during file transfer. I was so excited when modem speeds increased and achieved 56,000 bits per second transfer rates. I didn't think transfer rates could go faster, and I dreamed of a day when transfer speeds would be instantaneous.

It seemed that I enjoyed an endless amount of entertainment with the Commodore 64, and I worked during the summer picking strawberries and painting houses to make money to purchase games. Quickly getting bored with "old" games, I purchased as many new games as I could. When I didn't have money, I downloaded games from bulletin board systems. Bulletin board systems facilitated human-to-human interactions over a modem and telephone line before the Internet was available to consumers. I met an older gamer over the bulletin board system who wanted to trade games. He lived in my neighborhood, and we spent numerous days copying games and sharing copies of our games.

I spent significant amounts of time playing *Summer Games*, a track and field video game, rather than playing outside. *Summer Games* allowed me to dream about being an Olympian. I competed as a platform diver, pole-vaulter, swimmer, relay runner, gymnast, and skeet shooter. The game allowed me to imagine myself as a gold medalist. In the digital world, I could be Bruce Jenner or Carl Lewis.

My curiosity for the world of video games and computers grew. I loved the way the video games made me feel. I enjoyed being entertained and immersed in a fantasy world. I found excitement in being the main character of the story. The exploration of a new digital world was enticing and occupied my complete attention. The video games allowed me to live within and to explore a digital world much more complex and vast than the scenarios created by the *Choose Your Own Adventure* books I had loved to read as a child. The *Choose Your Own Adventure* books were popular for allowing the reader to feel as if he or she was the main character, making decisions that influenced the outcome of the story. I was always disappointed when the book ended, but video games were almost endless. I could play an adventure video game that seemed to last forever. My curiosity guided my thirsty mind into the new worlds of computers, programming, and video games. School was easy, and it bored me. Yet, the digital world was a challenge for me.

This curiosity is what attracts hundreds of millions of people to video games. It's a new universe to travel, a new puzzle to solve, a new task to achieve. By fulfilling the basic human need of curiosity, these games pull people in like magnets. When *Space Invaders* was launched, it was all about getting that high score and trying to develop a strategy to avoid the firing missiles. Even though it was a simple game, the exploration of a new digital world kept people playing for hours and hours at a time. But then, the game became more difficult. The aliens began moving faster and started closer to the player, forcing the gamer to adapt and keep coming up with new strategies for success. The game allowed a new world for the curious mind to explore, test, and conquer.

Similarly, in the game *Missile Command*, the player is trying to save a group of cities and protect them. As the player achieves new levels, it becomes more difficult to predict how the enemy will attack, so the strategy changes. These types of strategies in basic games make them very enticing; the more complex the game becomes, the more addictive the game becomes. As the digital world increases in complexity, the curious gamer becomes more immersed and eventually becomes hooked.

Looking at current games like the *World of Warcraft* or other massive multiplayer online role-playing games

(MMORPGs), the sense of curiosity is fulfilled because players are exploring new lands and new worlds. These MMORPGs are video games on steroids. With online games, players are exploring with other live players around the world. The social element magnifies the addictive nature. New dungeons and quests offer unique creatures with magical weapons or armor that characters can use, creating challenging and rewarding experiences for the player. These types of digital rewards signal the body to release endorphins into the bloodstream and feel-good dopamine into the brain. They tell the player, "this is fun," keeping them hooked into playing more and more.

Eventually, I enjoyed playing video games more than I enjoyed eating. Once, while shopping with my mom as a young child, I recall her giving me $10 to purchase lunch for myself. As I perused the menu at the deli, I noticed a *Missile Command* arcade machine. I cashed in the $10 bill for quarters and felt an adrenaline rush hearing the coins clink as they dropped from the change machine. I planned to play $2 worth of *Missile Command* and to save $8 for lunch. After playing eight games, I reasoned with myself that I didn't feel that hungry, so I fed another $3 into the machine. Eventually, I spent all $10 on *Missile Command*.

While sitting on a bench waiting for my mom, I felt anxious, guilty, and ashamed that I had spent the entire $10 on the game. My mom made less than four dollars per hour. I felt incredibly selfish wasting the entire amount feeding an arcade machine. I was hungry and without money for lunch; yet, still, I wished I had more money to advance past the last level that blew up all of my cities. I yearned for the euphoric rush of seeing the explosions and the excitement associated with hearing the game sounds.

Video game playing reinforces the neural pathways associated with addictive behavior. When a gambler is playing the slots, he might win sometimes, although he will lose most of the time. But video games are designed so that players will win most of the time. The big jackpots come when there is an in-game bonus or an enemy "drops" an item that is incredibly rare. If a player defeated the boss at the end of the quest, there may be a less than one percent probability of the boss dropping a rare item, so the player will have to defeat the boss over 100 times for that item. All players in MMORPGs seek to earn and keep magical armor, weapons, and items for their characters, helping their characters to be faster, stronger, or more powerful. The curiosity about the magical reward and how it will enhance play feeds the fundamental drive that draws in the player, engrossing them in the game.

The variable reward system, as seen in gambling and video games, strongly reinforces gaming behaviors. Research at Reed College showed students could be trained in specific tasks in video games utilizing an operant conditioning model similar to the ones performed on rats in the B.F. Skinner experiments.[5] Some gamers are so addicted that they experience serious physical and emotional withdrawal symptoms when forced to stop playing. Studies show that video game addiction is associated with depression, social phobias, and anxiety in children.[6]

Video game designers have recognized this need for curiosity and have developed the perfect business model: provide a huge digital fantasy world, facilitate online social interaction, give away the game for "free", and then rope gamers into paying a monthly subscription to keep playing. The *World of Warcraft*, for example, is a game with more than 11 million online subscribers who are paying an average subscription fee of $15 a month.[7] That's over $1 billion in annual revenue for just one game. In this way, video games continue to capture

5 NEURINGER ET AL., "COMPARING CHOICES AND VARIATIONS IN PEOPLE AND RATS: TWO TEACHING EXPERIMENTS." BEHAV RES METHODS INSTRUM COMPUT. 2000 AUG; 32(3): 407-16.Z
6 GORDON, SERENA. "VIDEO GAME 'ADDICTION' TIED TO DEPRESSION, ANXIETY IN KIDS." CBS NEWS. JANUARY 17, 2011. HTTP://WWW.CBS19. TV/STORY/13854944/VIDEO-GAME-ADDICTION-TIED-TO-DEPRESSION-ANXIETY-IN-KIDS. ACCESSED AUGUST 27, 2011.
7 IGN. "WORLD OF WARCRAFT: CATACLYSM." IGN PC. MAY 9, 2011. HTTP://PC.IGN.COM/ARTICLES/116/1166958P1.HTML. ACCESSED SEPTEMBER 11, 2011.

the curiosity of gamers around the world.

Chapter 3: Providing a Sense of Purpose in Life

After skydiving, Mark threw his parachute in the back of his truck. He put his car in gear and drove to the house he was renting from a friend. On the way home, his mind was focused on the new game he had recently purchased, one of the *Ultima* role-playing games. When he arrived at the house, he discovered that a container of antifreeze had leaked and soaked his parachute, so Mark decided to rinse off his gear in the bathtub. He turned on the water, added some mild detergent, and headed downstairs. His new video game in hand, he excitedly headed to the office and started installing the game onto the computer. As it was loading, he felt the familiar rush of adrenaline and excitement; he could hardly wait to dive into the new game. He carefully created a new warrior character and meticulously selected the qualities he wanted. He chose the weaponry and armor and planned how to acquire in-game gold to purchase the weapon and armor upgrades for his new character. Mark had built his ideal video game character—his avatar, his persona.

The game began, and Mark's character was venturing through a city. He visited the armory to shop for weapons and armor upgrades. Short on gold coins, he decided to delay upgrading his gear. He stocked up on healing potions, anticipating that he would need to heal after his battles. Then he meticulously double-checked his gear: sword, shield, leather armor, and supplies. He was soon led on a quest: to kill three trolls and report back to the town; it was a simple task to complete. Then he was called upon to complete the difficult quest of solving a mystery. He was heavily engaged in this mission until the faint sounds of water grabbed his attention. With a shock, Mark suddenly remembered that water was still running in the bathroom. He ran upstairs to find a waterfall cascading over the bathtub, running like a river straight into the air vents. Within a few minutes, Mark had successfully flooded a portion of his friend's house because he was so focused on his video game.

For many adults and children who are struggling with video game addiction, the lack of a true purpose in life is key to why they simply cannot kick the gaming habit. Therefore, the game they choose to play provides this sense of purpose, whether it's questing to find a magical item, seeking and destroying thugs, living in a digital world with an ideal digital partner, pursuing a dream career in a digital world, tending to a digital farm, or clearing a dungeon of all evil and then returning for a reward.

This digital reward system allows the brain to feel good. Gamers completing quests and tasks feel excitement, a sense of achievement, or a feeling of accomplishment due to the biochemical changes in the brain that release neurotransmitters controlling the release of hormones such as adrenaline, which speed up the heart rate and increase perspiration. These changes in the brain allow gamers to have the same sense of reward, same sense of real accolades they would feel if accomplished in real life. Gamers feel euphoric, and some describe the rush as being incredible when playing video games. For gamers who are goal-oriented, who are thrill-seekers, or who enjoy challenges, this sense of purpose helps fulfill them. For those who lack a sense of purpose in real life, video games give them a reason to live, a reason to have an identity, and a reason to have an ego, because the game provides a way for them to associate themselves with the avatar they've created in the game.

The "digital buffet" can fulfill the needs of anyone. Want to be a space traveler? Want to be a fantasy warrior or a magical character who can cast powerful spells? Want to be an archer? Want to imagine yourself as a beautiful woman who lives in a digital world who marries her perfect digital man in an extravagant wedding? There are games for virtually anyone seeking anything, many of them simulating real life. There are astronauts, marine snipers, mercenaries who fly spaceships, alien warriors, ideal families, and sports stars. Whatever a gamer can possibly imagine is available.

For example, gamers in *The Sims* play with multiple characters, guiding them on different career paths and relationship goals, ultimately controlling their destinies. Gamers can buy their characters' homes, find them jobs, manage their relationships, organize parties, and see them marry and have babies. Without realizing it, these gamers start living through the characters, giving gamers a sense of purpose by watching, managing, and controlling the digital characters' lives.

As an addict trying to hide my addiction, I needed more time to play alone, so I introduced my wife to *The Sims*, allowing me more time to play my own games. When my wife experienced her Sims character having a child, she called me to the computer with the same excitement and joy as when one of her friends had given birth to a real baby. My wife shared with me that she felt emotionally invested in the characters in *The Sims* because she had created them, selected their physical features, and decided on their personalities. She would be upset with the kids or with me when we played with her Sims character. She wanted us to play with our own Sims characters.

Everyday, I looked forward to coming home from work and playing a quick game before dinner. One evening, I started a game of *Starcraft*, hoping to beat my opponent in a fifteen-minute match. After thirty minutes, my wife called me to dinner. I yelled back that I'd be there in just a few minutes. My opponent was difficult to defeat, and I completely lost track of time. Two hours later, I ate a cold dinner alone, not an unusual occurrence.

With complete immersion and investment of attention in a video game, gamers aren't able to separate the time anymore. What was once a half hour of gaming becomes an hour, two, four, or eight hours at a time. Some addicted gamers will play all night, sleep all day, and neglect school and work.

As we researched this book, we learned about dozens of children and young adults who failed out of school or college due to excessive video game playing. On the *On-Line Gamers Anonymous* website (www.olganon. org) and other similar websites, there are thousands of stories documented of troubled and ruined lives due to excessive video game playing and video game addiction.

In the game *Second Life*, over ten million people spend real money to purchase virtual houses, virtual islands, virtual clothing, and virtual consumer items to live in a digital matrix referred to as "living on the grid." People are pursuing their ideal careers, developing their dream relationships, experiencing childbirth, and even having virtual sex, by controlling a keyboard and mouse in the digital world known as *Second Life*.

The digital world provides a purpose that may not be well defined or may not exist for the gamer in real life. Many people spend so much time in the video game *Second Life* that time devoted to the game exceeds the time spent with people and relationships in real life. Real marriages are destroyed as some pursue intimate relationships with their digital partners. Unfortunately, many of these fantasy relationships end horribly when the couples meet in real life. The same problems preventing these individuals from having healthy, real relationships are still present; thus, the gamers struggle with developing real relationships with their fantasy lovers.

In the documentary *Life 2.0*, Jason Spingarn-Koff illustrates how boundaries of real life are blurred and melded with the digital world of the video game *Second Life*. "Every day, across all corners of the globe, hundreds of thousands of users log onto *Second Life*, a virtual online world not entirely unlike our own. They enter a new reality, whose inhabitants assume alternate personas in the form of avatars—digital alter egos that can be sculpted and manipulated to the heart's desire, representing reality, fantasy, or a healthy mix of both. Within this alternate landscape, escapism abounds, relationships are formed, and a real-world economy thrives, effectively blurring the lines between reality and 'virtual' reality." [8]

8 *LIFE 2.0, HTTP://WWW.LIFE2MOVIE.COM/ 2010.*

For people who are struggling in life, whether it's at work, at home, or at school, it's easy for them to dive into these games and to discover a sense of purpose and self worth. Instead of spending time pursuing their dreams and achieving real meaning in their lives—which takes time and effort emotionally and physically—the video game addicts find it more pleasurable and inviting to be a part of the digital world and to fulfill the purpose that the game maker has for them. The gamers feel they are accomplishing something, even though the video game accomplishments are only digital. After spending a full day playing video games, most people have nothing to show for their efforts.

This complete immersion, which is the goal of every successful game, is much more powerful than a movie or a book, because gamers are made to feel like they're living in the game and that they actually are that avatar or leading character in the game. Much more enticing than a book or movie that has an ending, the most addictive games are never ending, insidiously luring the gamers into the digital world and reinforcing the behavior leading to video game addiction.

The gamers start exhibiting physical changes when they approach difficult situations in the game. Their hearts will begin to thump harder, their hands will get sweaty, and they will physically jump if they're startled by something that's happening in the game. Gamers are so immersed in the music, the colors, the lights, the complete and utter experience of it all that they feel like they are the warrior walking through a dark, musty dungeon ready to slay a creature from hell.

The game makers have succeeded if they make the player feel a sense of purpose in the video game. If the first thing a person wants to do when they come home is to flip on the computer and start a game, the game makers have succeeded. If the first thing they think of after finishing their chores or to-do list is to sit down and play a game, the game makers achieved their goal. Or if they neglect real life, like the gamer named Mark, who allowed an overflowing bathtub to flood his friend's home because he was so caught up in his game, the game makers have done what they've set out to do: attract, enchant, entertain, facilitate escape, and eventually suck the player into the digital world.

Chapter 4: Heightening a Sense of Invincibility

Four-year-old Jack lives near my home, and I have known his parents well for several years. His mother is a pediatrician, and his father is an eye surgeon. Jack's parents are extremely careful about how long he plays video games. In his house, video games as well as television time are highly regulated. Recently, his parents removed the television and games from the playroom. One day, Jack was playing with my four-year-old daughter in front of my house. He came to me and greeted me with, "Hi, Mr. Andy!" I greeted him back and decided to ask him about his hobbies. Although Jack's access to video games is highly restricted, he loves video games and speaks about them with enthusiasm.

"Jack, what do you like to do for fun?" I asked him.

"I love video games!" he responded.

"What's your favorite game to play?"

"LEGO Star Wars. It's the best game!"

"What do you like about it?"

"I get to kill the villain."

"Do you feel powerful?"

"Oh, yes, I feel powerful! I get to kill him, over and over and over again."

"What happens if he kills you?"

"It's no big deal. The game lets me restart and I get to try again."

Intrigued by Jack's response, I realized that I felt the same. When the game didn't go my way or if I experienced a premature death, the restart button allowed me a second chance to be successful. Real life, on the other hand, did not have a reset button. Consequently, it was depressing for me to face my real-life struggles in the research lab during graduate school and to deal with my troubled marriage. Being invincible in a game was far more enjoyable.

When a video game allows a player to have that sense of pseudo-death, or a near-death experience and then becoming god-like and conquering death, or resurrecting again when they die, the gamer feels a true sense of suspense, danger, and power. Whether they're in a death match, searching for enemies hiding in buildings to overtake and defeat, or killing evil creatures in a dungeon, there is a tension that pulses through the body; palms get sweaty, pupils get wider, and adrenaline is flowing so the gamer is pumped up, solely focused on the dangerous task at hand in the game.

While playing video games, a person experiences the release of adrenaline, hormones, and neurotransmitters into the body, increasing the sense of awareness so that the gamer is ready to either fight or run away. This is the same type of fear response a person gets when they are afraid of heights or if come into close contact with a wild, threatening animal. They will experience a heightened state of awareness, where everything around them seems to slow down and hyper-awareness takes over. Video games do the same thing, but the gamer is in a safe environment. They are able to experience multiple fight or flight responses in a day of playing, continuously receiving the reward of resolution that comes after such an experience. And what happens if a gamer fights and loses? They don't really die; they just resurrect. As little Jack said, "It's no big deal. The game lets me restart and I get to try again." Gamers are given this sense of almighty, god-like power.

We are constantly reminded about our fear of death.

As we get older and face the natural consequences of an aging body, our fear of death increases. That fear will often determine how we take risks, what goals and objectives we set in life, or the career paths we choose. Some people fear death less than others. That's why we have military personnel, police officers, or firefighters, for example. Yet, there are other people who fear death so much that they avoid things such as airplanes, snakes, or spiders at all costs.

As a physician, I see numerous patients face death because of illness. People respond differently to stress and terminal illness. Some people face death and excel until their very last breath. Others seek addictive behaviors to escape the reality of dying.

One of my physician colleagues has a sister-in-law, Susan, who is dying from advanced cancer. Susan plays a MMORPG all day long, almost every day. Susan is morbidly obese, isolated from her family and friends, and escapes into the digital world of video games. It's an escape from the realties of her cancer and her slowly dying body.

In real life, individuals are vulnerable and susceptible to human emotions, fears, and eventual death. But in the digital world of video games, there is no real death. In games, there is the ability to reset, to restart, or to resurrect a character. These video games, by removing the natural human fear of death, give players a sense of security, control, and fearlessness that boost their egos and make them feel like they are undefeatable super-heroes.

Some games give the players a sense of immortality and perfection. Men and women love the game *Second Life* where their digital avatars never become sick, do not age, and look digitally perfect. In *Second Life*, the digital avatars have everlasting life. *Second Life* allows complete immersion where people live a never-ending soap opera consisting of millions of cast members. But as soon as they unplug, they are brought back to reality. They're reminded that human lives are fragile. They're reminded that they will eventually die. They remember that they aren't heroes or indomitable forces to be reckoned with. They're reminded that they don't have complete control of everything happening in their lives. Is it any wonder that gaming addicts prefer the digital world?

Chapter 5: Feeding the Ego

Steve was an accomplished *Call of Duty* soldier. After he logged into the PlayStation Network, he was determined and focused on winning. He quickly checked for his friends. He even spent $50 of his own hard-earned money mowing lawns at $10 per yard to purchase a Bluetooth headset, allowing him to chat online and talk smack with other players. He carefully picked out his gear, examined his weaponry, determined the grenades he needed, and planned out his strategy during the week.

His parents limited his access to the game, only allowing him to play on the weekends for a few hours, but he spent many hours during the week focusing on his weekend battles. He watched YouTube videos on the latest strategies, read up on new ways to conquer the game, and, every day, all day long, he plotted what he was going to do on Friday evening when he would be allowed to play. At school, between classes and during lunch, he talked to other kids about the game. Steve found a way to feed his obsession with *Call of Duty*, even with limitations on playing time.

When Steve logged onto his PlayStation Network, he found literally hundreds of thousands of other players ready for death matches. The game paired them up in groups, and they prepared to go into battle—good against evil, squad against squad, nation against nation. Eyes fixated on the screen, Steve ran into the battlefield. He shook his handheld knife; he crawled on the ground finding sniper positions; he fired his weapon through glass, aiming to kill the enemy. He was concentrating to achieve kill streaks, allowing him the ability to launch special weapons. The adrenaline and endorphins surging through his body were potent. He wiped his sweaty hands on the side of his pants and continued to play with a sense of concentration that was rarely exhibited in his day-to-day activities—school and playing competitive soccer. If left alone, Steve would play all-day and late into the evening.

Before becoming obsessed with *Call of Duty*, Steve was bright and athletic. He maintained a solid 3.5 grade point average. He had a naturally athletic body and incredible hand-eye coordination. As Steve became more obsessed with *Call of Duty*, however, his school performance dropped and he underperformed on the soccer field. At the height of his excessive game playing, Steve was barely making a 3.0 grade point average and was not maintaining his physical fitness. Running and working out were difficult and tiring. School was boring, unlike the video game, which gave him a thrill of excitement that he could indulge in on a regular basis. The digital accolades and pixelated medals he received as a five-star general in the game superseded any real-life awards or recognition.

The desire to feed the ego is a basic human desire. Everyone needs an ego to have confidence, to maintain a positive self-image, and to be able to walk with head held high. Video games give players huge boosts to their egos because they are generals, kings, lords, beautiful, perfect, and can essentially play God.

In *Call of Duty*, for example, players can reach the five-star-general status quickly, but in real life a dedicated soldier In the U.S. military could serve forty years and never reach the rank of just a one-star-general. In-game achievements give the player a sense of complete control, power, and an incredible feeling of triumph. The digital ego, because it's controlled by the player, becomes frighteningly one with the player's real life ego.

When devoting too much time in the virtual world, the digital ego becomes one with the gamer's real-life ego, and he loses connection with real-world relationships, performs poorly in real-world jobs, and eventually suffers from depression when not playing the video game. If a person's ego is one with their digital ego, the addicted player only yearns to play more of the video game because that is where they feel good about themselves as their real-world life is deteriorating. Video game addiction is a vicious downward spiral into deep depression, shame, denial, increased hunger for the game, and the inability to stop playing.

Video games are a form of a digital drug that fills egos and makes people feel good. Because of the vast digital buffet of video games to choose from and the ability to easily access these games whenever and wherever people want, there will be a video game that appeals to every person and people may get hooked on them.

When I observe four-year-olds fighting over smart phones and tablets to play video games, I see the tragically addictive potential of these games. My four-year-old daughter fights with her friends to dominate game time to play *Angry Birds*. While playing the game, the focus they exhibit is intense and impressive. There seems to be an incredible sense of achievement and ego fulfillment when the kids play the game. These four-year-olds cheer with pride and excitement when advancing levels and knocking down structures.

I enjoyed defeating other players online in real-time strategy games like *Warcraft III* and *Starcraft*. I felt a great sense of accomplishment as I climbed the ladder of rankings, seeing my name at the top of the charts. I felt proud that I won significantly more games than I lost. By feeding the ego—even though the accomplishments were not real—I felt important, successful, and skilled. Unfortunately, this sense of success was not long lasting. I realized that when I left the game, I had real-life problems and real-life challenges to face. So, I had to play more to help me forget my real-life issues.

This form of digital escape drives gamers to reach for new achievements, new accomplishments, and new rewards within the video game to feel better. If a gamer doesn't continue to play, they likely feel lost, forlorn, depressed, and overwhelmed. To an addicted gamer, solving problems means running away from real-life issues and challenges by plunging back into the game.

Video game addiction is a rapidly growing problem at all colleges and universities. While waiting for a flight from San Diego to Baltimore, I met a computer science major, Brian, who said every student in his computer science department played numerous hours of video games during school. Several students performed poorly in their academic work because of playing more than thirty hours of video games a week. Some students required extra years of college to graduate. When I asked Brian why video games are so addictive, he answered, "There is nothing in life that provides the same rush and euphoria as video games."

I met a young woman at my friend's house recently. Lynn attends a highly prestigious university on the East Coast. Lynn said that all of her male friends play video games. They gather in groups, play all night, and play excessively. Lynn, a beautiful and intelligent woman, added, "I am frustrated because guys are too busy playing games and not pursuing women." Have games become more fun and more ego-boosting than dating attractive people? Are guys avoiding relationships with women by playing video games? Philip Zimbardo, PhD presents the argument that video games and Internet pornography are ruining an entire generation of boys in his article titled *The Demise of Guys*.[9]

There is always something more that the gamer can obtain in a video game that will bolster confidence, enhance the ego, and energize them in the digital world. For most of the online role-playing games, gamers strut their gear, armor, or weapons, and if they see that another gamer has "newbie," low-level gear, they won't include them in their group. Players feel rejected and have to upgrade their gear and play more to keep up with the levels of other players in the video game.

Therefore gamers keep up with the Joneses in the digital world by investing more hours into the video game

9 CNN HEALTH. 'THE DEMISE OF GUYS': HOW VIDEO GAMES AND PORN ARE RUINING A GENERATION. HTTP://WWW.CNN.COM/2012/05/23/HEALTH/LIVING-WELL/DEMISE-OF-GUYS/INDEX.HTML, MAY 25, 2012. ACCESSED ON MAY 25, 2012.

or even paying real money to enhance their characters. A video game addict invests an incredible amount of time and often money to make their avatar, their digital persona, more powerful so they feel included and regain that sense of ego. In essence, these multiplayer, online games trap players. They can't just play casually, because there is enormous peer pressure to continually attain and realize excellence in the video game. When an addicted player suffers from low self-esteem, stress, or any other types of emotional issues, the digital world provides an environment for instant ego fulfillment.

Chapter 6: Offering Companionship

I went to Reed College and didn't play video games except when I had extra quarters for pinball machines in the student lounge. For one, I didn't have access to a gaming computer. My Macintosh SE was not an ideal gaming computer with its black and white monitor and limited game selection. I had left all of my video game consoles at my parents' home, knowing that I didn't need distractions during college. I was focused on getting into medical school because I wanted to escape the poverty I had experienced as a child. In addition, I enjoyed working with people, I loved the medical sciences, and I had a strong desire to help others feel better.

My determination during college paid off as I received six full-ride scholarships to medical schools through the Medical Scientist Training Program, a combined MD-PhD degree program supported by the National Institutes of Health. Three of the scholarships were from top ten medical schools. I received full tuition and an annual stipend for living expenses. I decided to pursue my medical training at The Johns Hopkins University, School of Medicine where I would focus on earning my medical degree to be a surgeon and a doctoral degree in neuroscience.

I researched the molecular biology and neurobiology of learning and memory and how these neural pathways are damaged in neurodegenerative diseases, such as Alzheimer's.

The MD-PhD program was an eight-year program divided into two years of medical school, four years of graduate school, and two years of clinical rotations. Medical school was easy because I had a strong science and research background from Reed College. I didn't have to devote significant time to studying to pass my tests in medical school. As a medical student, I was bored during the first two basic science years.

The life of a PhD graduate student, on the other hand, was isolating. I worked in my corner of the lab, poured my gels, worked on my DNA sequences, and planned experiments. In graduate school, the project determined whether or not I graduated or failed. Most of the time, the project that I worked on was mine alone; it was my doctoral thesis. Graduate students at Johns Hopkins were pushing the envelope of science and continually contributing to advancements in medicine and research. It was not uncommon to work alone, for long hours in the lab. Biomedical research was extremely isolating.

My wife and I met during junior high school but did not pursue a romantic relationship until college. She moved to Baltimore, Maryland to be with me, and we were married during my third year at Johns Hopkins. We had infant children and my wife worked twelve to fourteen hours a day as a nurse at Johns Hopkins; because many of her shifts were at night, days would go by and I wouldn't see her at all.

I have great respect for parents who take care of young children, because it can be lonely. Adults with young children yearn for other adult interaction, conversation, and intellectual stimulation. While my wife was still working, I was the primary provider for my infant son and daughter after picking them up from daycare. During the day, I was isolated in the lab. During the evening, I was isolated caring for my infant children. This made it very easy to be drawn to the Internet, where the digital world allowed me social interaction with other adults. With just a few clicks of a button, I could be put in touch with other people through video games, such as *Warcraft II*, *Starcraft*, *Diablo*, *Ultima Online*, or *Asheron's Call 2*. People interacted with my character, named MudPhud for MD-PhD, and asked me about my day. I felt kinship, camaraderie, and companionship.

After a long day at the lab, when things had been frustrating for me, I went home to dive into video games to escape. Similar to when I was a young child, I utilized video games to fulfill basic emotional needs and to be entertained. After the house was quiet and boredom began to set in, I turned to my guild in *Ultima Online*, one of the first generation MMORPGs. My *Ultima Online* guild consisted of members who played together, socialized together, and provided support for each other while advancing through the game. It was wonderful. I felt part of a team. I was accepted. I no longer felt alone because I could chat and talk online to other adults.

While my infant son slept in a baby carrier next to my computer, I was transported into a new world that kept me entertained, engaged, and challenged throughout the night. The immersion into the digital world of *Ultima Online* helped me to escape my daily grind as a graduate student and the stress of supporting a young family. The video game facilitated my social interaction with other people without requiring me to leave my apartment.

The Internet allows instant access to millions of people around the world. The *World of Warcraft* is estimated to have over eleven million subscribers. The world of *Second Life* is estimated to have twenty million accounts created with nearly ten million people actively involved in that game. These games, among others, provide intrigue, camaraderie, and companionship for players. In the game *World of Warcraft* for example, players are able to emote real feelings. The *World of Warcraft* "toon"—slang for avatar or character—bows, waves, flirts, laughs, cries, and performs a myriad of other social interactions on the computer screen. If a gamer loves, hates, or likes someone, the character is able to act out these emotions. There are players who associate their real identities with their toons.

In the modern, busy world where people feel isolated and are unattached with no community to call their own, there is a longing to fit into a group of people with whom they can relate and connect. The need for companionship is easily fulfilled with Internet games and MMORPGs. This is apparent in the game *Second Life*, where the user dictates the design, look, and feel of the digital world. The users create homes, islands, and exotic locations. In this fantasy game, people are finding their online companions and ideal digital partners. Some even get married, buy houses, and have children together, all while their real-life spouse sits in the other room at home.

It may sound odd, but this type of other life is more common than you might think. It's similar to escaping with movies or books. When my wife viewed *Second Life* gameplay videos on YouTube, she said with intrigue, "Wow, this seems fun. It's like living in a soap opera." As readers or moviegoers, people are immersed in a story line, but in video games, the game makers create a much more complex, interactive world in which men and women can engross themselves. Gamers are the main characters in a never-ending story. They create their ideal selves, choosing whatever hairstyle, hair color, skin color, body shape, and other features they wish they could have. With these perfected avatars and the confidence anonymity provides, digital world companionship is incredibly common and easy to foster.

It's easy to have charisma and confidence online, even if they're lacking in real life. These relationships and companionships that are formed online are very temporary, however. They're not strong and secure; they are short-lasting relationships that can easily disappear at a moment's notice. If another player decides they're tired of the game and stops playing, that relationship is immediately over. If the video game company discontinues the video game, then the virtual world disappears. This is shocking and upsetting to addicted gamers, resulting in shame, frustration, anger, and depression.

Every hour that a gamer spends online is one hour that could have been invested in a solid, long-lasting relationship in real life. These players shift their priorities from the real world to the digital world, and as a result, these players are building relationships on a weak foundation. People are destroying relationships in the real world because of their devotion to the digital world and isolation while they "live" in the digital world. They feel there's no other choice except to keep going back to the gaming world. It's a vicious cycle.

Chapter 7: Satisfying the Need for Challenges

My father and brother both have bipolar disorder, also known as manic depression, causing them to have severe mood swings. For months they are hyper, rarely sleeping; and then they drop down to severe depression, sleeping most of the day, only to repeat the cycle again and again. Unlike my father and brother, I am able to focus my thoughts. I have not developed bipolar disorder, and I am able to successfully complete projects with robust energy and passion. I appear to be hypomanic because I can work effectively and energetically for several days and weeks with extremely few hours of sleep, an attribute that has allowed me to succeed as a physician and in business.

During graduate school, my ability to function on few hours of sleep proved useful in fueling my excessive and addictive video game playing. My wife compared me to a toddler. I worked and completed tasks throughout the day with intense energy and determination, only to crash and fall asleep around 9 p.m. After four to five hours of sleep, I was awake and ready to go again. During the middle of the night, Internet gaming provided continual stimuli and challenges, allowing my energy to be expended in the digital world.

One morning, I awoke after sleeping a few hours following a twelve-hour gaming session. As I logged on to Battle.net, Blizzard's online gaming network, I felt the adrenaline rushing through my body. My heart raced, and I was eager to play a *Warcraft III: Reign of Chaos* ladder match. I was within reach of advancing within the top 100 players on Battle.net. The game matched me with another player, and we were transported to a random map where our one-on-one battle would take place. The winner would advance up the ladder ranking, and the loser would drop in ranking.

I quickly examined the map and assessed the possible starting locations for the other player. I studied my location and prepared the battle plan. While planning my attack strategy, I directed my online workers to collect gold and lumber, resources required to build buildings and assemble troops. The faster my workers collected resources, the quicker I could build an army to defeat my opponent.

After wiping my sweaty palms on the side of my pajama bottoms, I clicked on the peasant who was chopping wood, and he said, "Yes, me lord?" Amused by the audio response of my peasant worker, I felt powerful and in command. I was the army commander for the Human Alliance. After thousands of hours devoted to the game, I felt some emotional attachment to the digital characters I controlled. I was delighted by their animations and audio responses. I was directing and micromanaging my workers and growing army. I had a good start, and I felt confident that victory favored me in this game.

As I was commanding my workers to gather resources to build farms and barracks for troops, I did not know what my opponent was doing, because I could not see beyond the edge of my base due to the "fog of war." I continued creating farms and barracks, carefully maintaining an optimum ratio of them to the peasants. I created my first three ground units called footmen. As I planned my strategies on how to advance and to attack my opponent, I contemplated rushing with footmen versus upgrading to knights, or possibly creating air-units.

Suddenly I was ambushed by three grunts, the Orc equivalent of my footmen. It was a three-on-three battle. My opponent had the upper hand, the element of surprise. The grunts concentrated their attack on one footman and quickly killed him. It was now a three-on-two battle. I rallied my peasants to arm themselves as militia, but my opponent was stronger, and soon these three grunts killed my footmen. Two more grunts arrived as reinforcements, and the Orc army began to wreak havoc on my militia, annihilating my peasants and destroying my newly created barracks and farms. The game was over. My heart was racing. My palms were sweaty.

My lips were quivering. I was frustrated and full of rage. I was defeated, and my ranking dropped on Battle.net. Yelling profanity at the computer screen, I manically prepared for another battle.

When video games were first introduced on consoles and computers, they were entertaining because of the artificial intelligence programmed into them. But the old generation games became less popular when the Internet offered a completely new and enticing gaming environment—one that allowed the human mind to compete with another human mind, something with which no computer at the time could compete. Knowing that a human player was my opponent in a video game, I felt nervous, excited, and tense during the match. Being defeated by a human player elicited emotions of anger, frustration, and even depression. Achieving victory over another human player provided an incredible rush of euphoria, excitement, and ego boost. It was the challenge of playing other people that was the irresistible draw to Internet gaming during the height of my video game addiction.

One of my favorite video games was *Warcraft II: Tides of Darkness*. We used a program called *Kali* to network computers over the Internet, allowing gamers to play other people living around the world in games that would normally only be played at local area network

(LAN) parties. In these LAN parties, people brought their computers to people's homes and gamed together in one room. By using *Kali*, we were able to use the Internet to network our computers, playing with thousands of other players while never leaving our homes. We were in complete isolation from the real world.

Warcraft III: Reign of Chaos was the third installment of the Warcraft video games and allowed multi-player, Internet play. *Warcraft III* provided me with an incredible challenge. Although I had played thousands of hours of the game previously, it had taken a player I did not know less than five minutes to defeat me with a well-executed three-grunt rush. In that short amount of time, through skill and dedication to the game, he had created three ground troops that attacked and overtook me.

I went back to determine exactly how the player had beaten me by viewing replays. Then I practiced to improve my game. The next time, I was able to defeat my opponent and was instantly filled with a boosted ego and a rush of adrenaline. As gamers were climbing up the ranking ladder, perfecting their battle skills and scheming up new strategies, these five to ten minute matches became more and more frequent, easily turning into hours and sometimes all-night gaming competitions.

These games provided me with an unlimited amount of challenge. There is always going to be someone better than you, more skilled in the game than you. There will always be a ranking system and groups where your scores are compared and where you're continually challenging yourself to beat the other person, to get more points, to advance in the game, and to become higher ranked. Anyone who is interested in a challenge can be sucked into the gaming world. People want to be successful. People want to be tested. People play games that challenge them mentally and allow strategy innovation. Numerous gamers have told me that the euphoria associated with playing online games is unmatched by other activities in real life.

One of my colleagues went to a premier engineering school in the northeastern part of the United States. In his fraternity, over half of the students played five to six hours of video games a day. There were times when these students would discuss with one another how they were expected to be the next up-and-coming leaders in engineering, developing new ideas. The students proposed that they stop playing video games, but the games were much more fun and challenging to play. They continued playing games. Five to six hours a day of video games add up to thirty-five to forty-two hours a week, while the average college student spends only seven to twelve hours a week studying for classes according to the 2003 Pew Internet & American Life Project.[10]

When I was in college, I did not study more than twenty hours a week. This is a huge disproportion. Five to six hours a day spent on video games could be time devoted to innovation in a chosen field, to getting better grades in school, to starting a business, or to learning new skills to be more competitive after college. Spending thirty-five to forty-two hours a week on games is like having another full-time job. There are marketing tactics where game companies hand out consoles for free to college students if they buy a computer. Once the company gets the console in the individuals' hands, students use the company's online gaming network and digital products and purchase software to use the console. These video game companies know that people are hooked on games.

Dr. Nick Yee gathered data from 3,000 MMORPGs players through online surveys and reported that there are three major types of motivations to play online: (1) achievement in the game, (2) social interaction, and (3) immersion in the virtual world.[11] Dr. Yee's study also showed that specific motivations to play online were

---

10 JONES ET AL., "LET THE GAMES BEGIN: GAMING TECHNOLOGY AND ENTERTAINMENT AMONG COLLEGE STUDENTS." PEW INTERNET & AMERICAN LIFE PROJECT. 2003.
11 YEE N. "MOTIVATIONS FOR PLAY IN ONLINE GAMES." CYBERPSYCHOL BEHAV 2006; 9: 772–775.

associated with negative consequences resulting from online gaming.

I understand firsthand the addictive potential of *World of Warcraft*, a game that resulted in my relapse from video game abstinence. I stopped my pathological forty to fifty hours per week of game playing in 2004. I was doing well in my career as an ophthalmologist, an eye surgeon and a physician. Three years later, a colleague placed a CD-ROM of *World of Warcraft* on my desk, a game I had been avoiding because I had played similar MMORPGs in the past and I knew their addictive potential. I thought I could control my game playing because I had not played games for over three years, but I was wrong.

One hour a night quickly turned into two, then four, and then all night. I always felt shame after an all-night gaming session, knowing that my commute to work would be hell. Driving after playing all night was scary. I found myself nodding off at the wheel and even hallucinating while entering and leaving a hypnagogic state associated with falling asleep. Occasionally, I was so tired that I had to find a gas station or a parking lot where I could nap before I continued my commute. I learned the reality that, similar to drug abuse and other behavioral addictions, once an addict, always an addict. Alcoholics cannot socially drink. Cocaine addicts cannot occasionally use coke. Video game addicts cannot control their gaming. I devoted more than 1,400 hours over a period of one year in the *World of Warcraft*.

When an addict starts abusing a substance, he or she will try to get other people hooked, too, in order to help justify the addiction. Thus, I introduced my wife to *The Sims* and eventually got my kids to play *World of Warcraft* with me as well. I knew I was spending less time with my family and that I was slipping back into my addictive behavior, so I tried to control my hours of playing and justify the time playing with my kids as "quality time." I was lying to myself. I played too much. I was angry with my kids when they didn't play the way I wanted them to play, and I encouraged them to collect resources in the game so I could make virtual gold, a process referred to as "money farming." I even paid $100 for virtual gold so I didn't have to farm the gold myself. I needed the virtual gold to upgrade my toon's armor and weapon.

One day while playing with my son, I said, "Son, you can play *World of Warcraft*, but I want you to play only in this region of the map. Your goal is to collect copper ore when you see it. We need to sell the ore in the auction house for gold coins to get better weapons and armor."

"Okay, Dad. Got it," my son said excitedly.

Thirty minutes passed.

"What are you doing?!" I yelled at him. "I told you to stay in this region of the map because that's where there is the most copper ore. I never gave you permission to explore! Can't you ever follow directions?! Do I always have to watch over you? If you can't follow directions, then get off the damn game!"

Tears pooled in my son's eyes, "Yes, Dad."

Games like the *World of Warcraft* are designed to be addictive because the business model depends on the acquisition of players, the retention of players, and generation of a monthly subscription fee. It is estimated that *World of Warcaft* generates nearly two billion dollars in annual revenue. In order to generate this type of revenue, MMORPGs provide achievement, social interaction, and immersion in the virtual world. Achievements are awarded when players complete challenges in the game. Immersion occurs when the players feel they are a part of the digital world. My friends, who had never played video games before, became hooked on *World of Warcraft*. I recruited a physician friend, Jason, to play with me. I recall the excitement in Jason's voice after I assisted his hunter in training a pet in the game. He loved the challenges in the game and the ability to acquire a pet. Jason played more than I did over a period of two years. Jason's wife, to this date, cringes when I mention the game.

Video game addiction has become a rapidly growing and viral problem for youths and adults today. Their needs for challenges are not being met in the usual ways at school, at home, and in real life, so instead they turn to video games that stimulate them intellectually. Consequently, they are losing sight of what's important. Gamers who play in excess are putting their futures at risk.

Chapter 8: Gratifying the Desire to Be a Leader

Our guild, clad in red capes and full-plate armor, was determined to overtake and dominate the *Ultima Online* servers. This was during the beta test of the game for a limited number of *Ultima* fanatics. Our guild was over fifty members strong and was used to playing together in the game *Warcraft II: Tides of Darkness*. In order to gain power, our guild needed plate armor and weapons. In the digital world of *Ultima Online*, the quickest way to arm the guild was to delegate jobs to individual guild members. I was appointed guild leader and entrusted with the guild's resources.

In order to create armor and weapons for the guild, the guild needed a grandmaster blacksmith. Determined to achieve the skill level of grandmaster blacksmith, I devoted over forty hours honing my crafting skills. But to achieve this title, I needed a lot of ore. I organized an ore train that mined ore from the mountains, far from the city. In order to maximize the carrying of ore, dozens of avatars stripped themselves of unnecessary weight and wore only their virtual undergarments. There was a pilgrimage of determined avatars in their underwear, each controlled by a human being, walking from the city to the mines in the mountain and back.

Suddenly, our workers were attacked by a rival guild. The guild chat window was flooded with profanity and requests for help. The entire guild was on high alert, and we all shared an urgency to organize and attack. By the time we arrived at the location of the ambush, the culprits had fled and were nowhere to be found. All of the ore our guild members had carried was stolen.

We rallied a team of guards to protect our ore train. The coordination of the ore train security force in tandem with me as the blacksmith was no small feat. Our guild had to log on at the same time and had to play literally all night. After melting ore to ingots and using the ingots to create armor and weapons, I was able to outfit the entire guild with plate armor and weapons. We used our strength and army to go outside the town and dominate anyone who walked by us, casting lightning spells to kill our victims and steal their belongings. We gained incredible power and wealth and had epic battles with rival guilds, fighting to achieve server dominance. My guild purchased virtual castles and special items with our virtual wealth. My leadership skills proved useful in the *Ultima Online* digital world. The *Ultima Online* MMORPG provided an unbelievable rush, and one that allowed me to act out a fantasy with other people while experiencing the satisfaction of leadership, control, and power.

Online games allow people to organize into social groups and guilds, affording them the ability to become leaders. In the game *World of Warcraft*, gamers can be leaders of a five-member group, organizing an adventure through a dungeon, or leaders of a much larger raid with a task to clear an advanced level dungeon. They can become guild masters, in charge of hundreds of people, or assistant guild masters. This allows for an interesting dynamic. The games mimic real life in that there are hierarchies of leadership positions to which players can aspire. For some, this provides an escape; for others, it provides a sense of accomplishment. For this reason, many gamers feel compelled to keep playing. For some, the need to lead is incredibly strong.

I was born a natural leader. I have charisma, drive, and the ability to influence other people to join my cause. In ninth grade, I ran for class vice president, and my friend, Matt, ran for class president. I recruited the entire cheerleading squad to make "Vote for Andy Doan" posters, and I recruited the popular jocks to support me. We wallpapered every available space with "Vote for Andy Doan" propaganda. I won the election by a landslide.

While not everyone has the same desire to lead, we are all called to lead at different levels in our homes, communities, businesses, and around the world. When real life does not present opportunities for leadership, however, natural leaders can feel frustrated and unfulfilled. When we turn to the digital world, we get to experience leadership opportunities in teams, guilds, and clans.

For many gamers engrossed in the online world of MMORPGs, there is peer pressure to complete the task at hand and to spend hours with the guild in order to accomplish these tasks. For those addicted to video games, the hours spent in the virtual world come at an incredible price—in school or work performance, real-life relationships, and health.

One gamer ignored the pain from a kidney stone and blood in her urine in order to finish a raid with her guild that lasted hours. Upon finishing the raid, she finally drove to the hospital alone, late at night. Another gamer played at least five hours of *World of Warcraft* every day, despite his job as a highly paid executive for a major software company. On New Years day, he played more than eighteen hours of *World of Warcraft*. The next day, his partner came down to see why he hadn't come to bed yet, only to discover that he had passed away sitting at his desk. *World of Warcraft* was still running. The autopsy showed that he had died from a massive pulmonary embolism, a blood clot from his leg that had traveled to his lungs and blocked the pulmonary circulation. He had no known medical issues that would have led to a pulmonary embolism. Dehydration from drinking on New Year's Eve, combined with being sedentary while playing a video game for more than eighteen hours, may have been the lethal combination.

Tens of thousands of women are complaining on *World of Warcraft* widows websites about husbands who are mesmerized in front of their computers, many playing twenty-five to thirty-five hours and more weekly. A friend of mine is a marriage counselor who says that excessive video game playing is an increasing problem observed in troubled marriages. Wives have wished that they were a keyboard and mouse because computers receive the most attention from their husbands. They cannot compete with their husbands' needs for power and leadership.

For some gamers in real life, they may not have the right combination of skills to become successful leaders, whether it's at work, school, or even at home. But online games can provide them with the feelings of power and leadership that they crave. These gamers feel able to surmount countries, to assemble armies, and to direct troops to achieve their conquest. With online gaming, there are abundant opportunities for power, supremacy, and control.

Internet gaming with other people increases the fun, attraction, and addictive potential to video games. While playing MMORPGs like *Ultima Online* and *World of Warcraft*, I was able to experience the exhilaration and power of leading an army to war in the digital world. Real people interacting with other real people in these role-playing games provide an incredible sense of team-work and fighting for a common goal. Gamers may lead their teams to victories, gratifying their desires to be leaders. Even though the leadership experience is solely online in the digital world, to the person playing an immersive game, it feels the same as if he were living it in real life. Video games allow people to feel important—like they matter—and that they can actually become the leaders they desire to be.

Chapter 9: Fulfilling Sexual Fantasies

In the 2007 *Wall Street Journal* article "Is This Man Cheating on His Wife?" journalist Alexandra Alter told a story of Ric Hoogestraat, a fifty-three-year-old man who sat at a computer more than ten hours a day while his wife, Sue, watched television in the next room.[12] Ric chatted online with a tall, slim redheaded avatar. In the video game known as *Second Life*, he controlled an avatar resembling his younger self, a burly man with a long gray ponytail, thick sideburns and a salt-and-pepper handlebar mustache. The real version of Ric had chronic health problems and required surgery. But the digital version of Ric was young, vibrant, and able to do things in the game that Ric could no longer do in real life due to his physical limitations. The redheaded avatar was controlled by 38-year-old Janet Spielman, a divorced mother of two.

These types of relationships in the digital world are common occurrences. As people pair up with their ideal digital companions, real-life spouses are abandoned. Sitting alone, Ric's real wife said, "Basically, the other

12 ALTER, ALEXANDRA. "IS THIS MAN CHEATING ON HIS WIFE?" WALL STREET JOURNAL ONLINE, AUGUST 10, 2007. HTTP://ONLINE.WSJ.COM/PUBLIC/ARTICLE/SB118670164592393622.HTML. ACCESSED AUGUST 26, 2011.

person is widowed. This other life [*Second Life*] is so wonderful; it's better than real life. Nobody gets fat, nobody gets gray. The person that's left can't compete with that."

To do research on *Second Life*, I created an avatar in the game. I wandered in and one of the first things I noticed was that the digital world of *Second Life* was a very socially interactive environment. People were chatting and establishing relationships with their avatars. Nearly all of the avatars looked perfect and beautiful. Women were represented with curvy bodies and digitally perfect, attractive features. Men were represented as muscular and digitally handsome. It seemed to me very easy to become emotionally attached with a *Second Life* avatar. I quickly noticed that the offer of opposite-sex companionship and pornography was widely available in the game. Walking into the "Red Light District" in the game, I found myself surrounded with virtual escorts, strip bars, and genitalia attachments in order to experience virtual sex.

The combination of sex and pornography in a video game has the potential for explosive growth and has already proven to become so. In *Second Life*, it's reported that there are over twenty million accounts, with more than half of those being active gamers. In the game, there are people making significant amounts of real money by providing a virtual escort service, and some are making six-figure incomes.[13] By day, a woman could be a mother and a lawyer, or some other professional. But by night, she might be the voice behind an avatar that charges twenty dollars an hour for a man to have virtual sex. While living in the game, otherwise known as "living on the grid," individuals purchase genitalia and "sex beds" so their avatars can have virtual sex with each other. People spend real money for virtual sexual experiences in the digital world of *Second Life*.

Per minute rates for phone sex could be as low as eighty-five cents, making an hour on the phone cost over fifty dollars. But in the virtual world of *Second Life*, where escorts charge only twenty dollars an hour, gamers not only have auditory stimuli, but also visual stimuli, making virtual sex less expensive and more appealing.

Excessive video game playing is hindering relationships and marriages, leaving little room for gamers to foster healthy relationships and sex lives with their real-life spouses and partners. Video games are increasingly cited as a reason for divorce. For example, it is reported that in the United Kingdom about fifteen percent of the divorce filings citing "unreasonable behavior" are due to excessive video game playing.[14] It is arguable that video

---

13 CBS NEWS, "THE STEAMIER SIDE OF SECOND LIFE." YOUTUBE. 2008. HTTP://WWW.YOUTUBE.COM/WATCH?V=RUMI3MAGKVC. ACCESSED AUGUST 27, 2011.
14 GAMEPOLITICS.COM, "EUROGAMER DIGS INTO DIVORCE ONLINE VIDEO GAME CLAIMS," MAY 31, 2011. HTTP://WWW.GAMEPOLITICS.

game addiction is unlikely to be the only factor resulting in broken marriages. On the other hand, it is also likely that excessive video game playing may be a mechanism for escape from real-life marital problems. The addictive behavior can be a manifestation of root causes discussed in this book, such as the need for challenge, ego-seeking behavior, and the desire for companionship, in addition to the hunger for sex.

As computer graphics improve, the pictures within the game begin to look more real. Future technology offers the ability to experience 3D images, surround sound, body suits, and tactile stimuli so the gamer can be completely immersed in the digital world. As games develop better graphics, they can turn into outright pornography, with players as the main characters in a porn flick.

In *Second Life*, the digital partner is always ready, willing, and able. Digital partners do not offer excuses and are rarely tired, because if they are logged in then they are ready to play. This is supposed to be only an entertaining video game environment, yet there are people who act out real sexual fantasies through the game. Gamers may tell themselves it's not real and that there's nothing wrong with connecting with other characters online in this way. However, admitted or not, these players, through their avatars, are forging emotional

COM/2011/05/31/EUROGAMER-DIGS-DIVORCE-ONLINE-VIDEO-GAME-CLAIMS. ACCESSED JUNE 21, 2011.

connections with one another and leaving less room for real-life relationships. While I never developed romantic relationships online, the guys in my guilds, including myself, would get excited hearing a female voice in the group. I would imagine what she looked like based on her voice, making me feel strangely aroused.

People who have left *Second Life* state that the sexual degradation in the game, the sexually deviant fantasies, and the way people sometimes treated them hurt their self-esteem and severely wound them emotionally. For others seeking companionship, the realistic graphics and interactive digital world facilitated a sense of love online.

As one gamer described her experience with *Second Life*: "I didn't even touch on the level of extreme depravity that exists there. I mean, very scary stuff, and the individuals actively participating in the rape scenarios, S&M, submissive/dominance, stripping, prostitution, and slavery may have serious real life issues. There is no limit to how low you can sink in *Second Life*. Matter of fact, it's almost become the norm and a hotbed of this kind of activity. I was hit on nearly every day and some of it was so inappropriate I felt uncomfortable and dirty in real life. I uncovered men posing as women and women posing as men. Like I stated in my earlier post, lying is rampant and the worst part is you actually invest real human emotions."

Sex has many purposes—pleasure, the ability for emotional and physical connection, and, of course, to have children. For some couples, having children is not possible, and this is a devastating blow to their goals and lifelong dreams. In a virtual world, couples who aren't able to have children or are past the point of having children, are able to purchase virtual pregnancies, where they can watch their avatar get pregnant, develop, and undergo virtual childbirth. Individuals select the type of pregnancy, such as single child, twins, or triplets. They also select hair color, eye color, and physical characteristics of their new baby. In the digital world, people can have their perfect digital baby.

Searching YouTube for "second life childbirth" produces numerous videos of people sharing their virtual childbirth experiences. As I watched these videos, I could see the lure of the *Second Life* digital world. People are living out their fantasies; they are living the soap opera instead of watching it.

Chapter 10: Meeting the Need for Love and Acceptance

For months, Jennifer had been withdrawing from her real-world family and friends. She had stopped being social and had even stopped being intimate with her husband. Instead, she had been pouring her time, emotions, and energy into her online avatar in *Second Life*. She was drawn to the game because she could flirt, adopt a different persona, and be accepted. She began interacting with one character in particular. What started out as innocent flirting led to an online relationship that included late night chats, e-mails, and phone calls. Jennifer had even become jealous when she observed her online lover interacting with other female avatars. She spent time fantasizing about leaving her real-life husband, getting a divorce, and moving in with her virtual online partner. Jennifer felt loved and accepted in the digital world. She could become the person she wanted to be in the digital world of *Second Life*. She was completely captivated by the game and how it made her feel. *Second Life* had sucked her in.

Eventually, Jennifer became devastated when she realized that she had pushed all of her real relationships to the side and lost most of them. And although she had fantasized about it, she was distraught when she grasped the fact that she was on the verge of losing her marriage, too. Jennifer started playing less of the game, but soon she experienced physical withdrawal symptoms and depression. She tried to reintegrate herself into the real world again, and she worked on her real marriage. She attempted to repair all of the troubled relationships she had created with her neglect. Looking back, Jennifer understood what an incredible waste of time, resources, and real-life opportunities her gaming habit had been.

The discussion forums on the *On-Line Gamers Anonymous* website, www.olganon.org, document hundreds of similar stories of men and women living in virtual worlds seeking love and acceptance, where they feel they are a part of an actual relationship. As a marriage mentor for our church and with my own marital problems during the height of my video game addiction, I know firsthand that marriage in real life can be tough; it takes work and devotion to make a marriage strong. But in the virtual world, it's easy. People select their ideal body characteristics to make themselves perfect; they choose their perfect career, and have, in essence, their dream world and dream relationship, free of any problems or challenges. This cycle is destructive, because it's nothing but a digital fantasy.

Take Derrick and Malia, a newly married couple who moved away from their friends and families. They knew very few people in their new town, and Malia found herself telling Derrick that it was fine to get online to play with his friends. He had been playing video games for years, and she loved her husband and wanted him to be happy. Feeling lonely, she also joined in and got trapped into the cycle of gaming every night for hours on end playing *World of Warcraft* with her husband.

Malia became addicted to the game and started falling behind at work and with real-life responsibilities. She was using the game to spend time with her husband in the digital world, but she realized that the in-game time was not quality time that built their relationship. The real draw to the digital world was not time together, but the game itself. She worried that they might be becoming addicts, so Malia decided to limit her playing to one hour a day. She started slowly falling behind in the game, since her husband and online friends were not limiting their playtime, and soon she quit playing altogether. She knew it was a full-fledged addiction when her husband continued to play excessively for an additional six months after she had left the video game. He was obsessed with it. He thought of the game when not playing. He played late every night and, at times, played through the night.

Malia confronted Derrick and told him that he was neglecting important aspects of his life. Derrick insisted that playing with his friends online was healthy and just the same as the way other groups of friends would hang out bowling or watching sports. She recognized that he was trying to rationalize his addictive behavior. It was wreaking havoc in her husband's life and carrying over into their marriage. By joining her husband in the video game, she was hoping to foster her relationship and seek love and acceptance from him, which worked initially. In the end, gaming together was damaging their marriage. Malia found herself alone in a new town, neglected by her new husband.

The need for affection and total acceptance drives many people to the digital world of video games. For example, if a person enters a game with desirable skills that are needed by a group, they are immediately wanted and accepted. In the real world, they may have just had a terrible day and are not feeling appreciated or acknowledged. But within minutes of logging onto a game, they are immediately ushered into a group and feel loved, needed, and accepted. This is what likely leads to online obsessions, whether it's with social networking or gaming online. In real life, individuals may rarely hear compliments about their looks or personalities; but on Facebook, similar social networking sites, or virtual online games, people are put in touch with hundreds, if not thousands, of people who can "like" who they are, what they look like, and what they're doing. Online, people can feel accepted, appreciated, and loved on a daily basis.

A study of 30,000 gamers conducted by Dr. Nick Yee, an expert in self-representation and social interaction in virtual environments, showed that nearly 40 percent of men and 53 percent of women who play online games said their virtual friends were equal to or better than their real-life friends. More than a quarter of gamers said the emotional highlight of the past week occurred in a computer world, according to the survey, which was published in 2006 by Massachusetts Institute of Technology Press's journal *Presence*.[15]

According to the U.S. 2011 Census, the majority of Americans use the Internet.[16] Nearly all young adults aged eighteen to twenty-nine years old (95 percent) use the Internet. About nine in ten Americans aged thirty to forty-nine years old are online (87 percent) and eight in ten Americans aged fifty to sixty-four years old utilize the Internet (78 percent). Even four in ten sixty-five year olds and over use the Internet (42 percent). The Census data

15 ALTER, ALEXANDRA. "IS THIS MAN CHEATING ON HIS WIFE?" THE WALL STREET JOURNAL. AUGUST 10, 2007. HTTP://ONLINE.WSJ.COM/ ARTICLE/SB118670164592393622.HTML. ACCESSED AUGUST 27, 2011.
16 U.S. CENSUS BUREAU. STATISTICAL ABSTRACT OF THE UNITED STATES. 2011.

show that about two in three (61 percent) of Internet users use social networking websites.

Perhaps the need for love and acceptance drives people to become obsessive about their use of social media websites such as Facebook. Facebook is available everywhere: on computers, mobile devices, and cell phones. It can be viewed as a social game where high scores are tallied by the number of friends a person accumulates and "likes" —a mechanism of denoting online peer approval—an individual acquires.

I have met people, particularly adolescents, who exhibit addictive behaviors when utilizing social networking websites. Let's consider Scarlet, a twelve-year-old entering adolescence, where hormones are surging and peer opinion plays a significant role in self-esteem. Scarlet experiences feelings of approval when her friends "like" her posts and comment on her photos in a positive way. I saw the joy and excitement in her eyes when she discussed the events on Facebook. She described Facebook events as if they were occurring in her real life, describing the teenage drama developing on her friend's wall and expressing anger when her friends, particularly her brother, tease her online. Facebook, for many people, is an extension of their real life social interactions. The frequency and volume of social interactions, however, are much higher online than in real life.

Online comments elicit an emotional response in people who receive them. When a friend compliments Scarlet on her attire at school, it results in a positive reinforcement of that behavior. The next time Scarlet selects an outfit, she will more likely choose the attire that received the most compliments. In real life, compliments and encouragements come occasionally. On Facebook, in contrast, Scarlet posts an activity, comment, or photo, and, almost instantly, there are old friends, new friends, and new acquaintances immediately connecting with her. People are commenting and "liking" her posts and photos. This can provide an incredible adrenaline rush. Even at the age of forty, I feel appreciated, accepted, and good when other people comment positively on my Facebook posts and photos. A quick "like" on my photos and comments make me smile because I know someone else appreciated my contribution.

But the obsessive behavior of always yearning to be on social media websites, and the significant time investment on these websites, can be viewed as a consequence of classic operant conditioning. We are subjects in the Skinner box. The lever is the computer and the rewards are the social media "likes" and positive comments from our friends. Those seeking acceptance and love can get lured into Facebook because the rewards they seek, such as social acceptance and love, are provided in rapid-fire fashion. The more social rewards they receive, the more time they invest, post, play, and interact on Facebook to gain increasing numbers of digital rewards.

From my personal experience, the relationships developed on Facebook are not as strong and meaningful as in real life; and yet, I can't help but feel affirmed when people, even old friends I haven't spoken to for years, leave comments such as, "I saw your vacation photos. I wished I could be there with you!" or, "You have such a beautiful family!" Conversely, when people ignore me, I feel hurt and rejected.

Unlike MMORPGs and other online games, Facebook offers a more attractive environment for those seeking love and acceptance. Many of the online friends who are providing us with digital rewards, such as virtual gifts, "likes", and kind comments, are actually our friends in real life. The positive reinforcements we receive from our real-life friends through social media are pleasing and meaningful. The combination of accessibility, rapid-fire endorsements, and our need for love and acceptance, can make social-media websites like Facebook highly addictive.

For example, when my wife turned forty, she posted on her Facebook wall, "So I am sort of feeling funky about turning the big 40. " Within moments, she received comments and support from her family and friends. Even the friends she had met while living abroad in England during high school responded with support. She was shocked by the number of posts made about her status. It made her feel loved and accepted. In discussing this with her, I observed a phenomenon of quantity versus quality associated with social media. To her, the online reward was less meaningful than face-to-face encounters. On the other hand, although she would feel extremely loved if her close friend from England were able to fly out and celebrate her 40th birthday in person, her friend could not be there, and so a Facebook comment enabled this friend to make at least a small emotional connection with her.

Social media websites facilitate high quantity of social interactions but less quality in the interactions. In contrast, real-life encounters require more time and emotional commitment, and people experience less quantity of real-life encounters than Facebook encounters. The face-to-face interaction, however, is more valuable as it is real and unfiltered.

My wife is not addicted to Facebook. However, for some Facebook users, it becomes disruptive in their lives, as the obsession to use social media is similar to other behavioral addictions.[17]

17 COHEN, ELIZABETH. "FIVE CLUES THAT YOU ARE ADDICTED TO FACEBOOK." CNN HEALTH. APRIL 23, 2009. HTTP://ARTICLES.CNN.COM/2009-04-23/HEALTH/EP.FACEBOOK.ADDICT_1_FACEBOOK-PAGE-FACEBOOK-WORLD-SOCIAL-NETWORKING?_S=PM:HEALTH. ACCESSED

People yearn for social interaction and connection. On the Internet, people enjoy the ability to control what information and images represent them to others, along with the rewards of personal connections with little risk and emotional investment. But because the quality of the online interaction is lower than real life, people must utilize social media in larger quantities and in greater frequency to feel accepted, to experience love, and to achieve happiness. Similar to the enticing lure of the digital world for gamers, social media is an incredible lure for those seeking approval and love.

As discussed in the introduction to this book, Shawn Woolley threw his whole existence into the digital world of *EverQuest*. Shawn searched for love and acceptance in the game world. He eventually withdrew from his real-life family and friends to spend more time with his online "friends" whom he never met face-to-face. He developed emotional bonds with new friends online that perhaps provided him with feelings of love and acceptance. And when an online character that he had connected emotionally with and had felt acceptance from rejected him, he felt true sorrow, pain, and anguish. Shawn was alone and isolated. He lost all connection to his real-life family and friends as well as to his online friends. His need for love and acceptance and his experience of rejection led to his suicide. The end result of people placing their hearts in virtual relationships is

AUGUST 27, 2011.

most often the breaking of those hearts.

Chapter 11: The Tetris Effect The Melding of Worlds

Six-year-old Sarah loved playing *Farmville* on Facebook. The cute little animals captivated her, and she proudly watched her garden grow. She enjoyed having the responsibility of tending to the pixilated crops and taking care of the animals.

One day, she was traveling with her parents in the car, and as they passed a large farm, they saw a herd of sheep grazing in the field. Sarah raised her hand to the window and bent her index finger like she's clicking the button on a computer mouse and innocently said to her mother, "Mommy, I wish there was a button on the sheep that I could click on so I could harvest them." Sarah's young mind was already melding the digital world with the real world.

When my daughter was eight years old, she loved playing with *Webkinz*. *Webkinz* was launched in 2005, and at one point it attracted nearly four million active users.[18] *Webkinz* created cute stuffed animals for kids and pro-

---

18 SNOW, BLAKE. "GIGAOM TOP 10 MOST POPULAR MMOS." GIGAOM. JUNE 13, 2007. HTTP://GIGAOM.COM/2007/06/13/TOP-TEN-MOST-POPULAR-MMOS/. ACCESSED JULY 15, 2011.

vided each toy with a unique identification number. My daughter lived through her stuffed animals' lives online through the *Webkinz* MMORPG portal. She was able to control her digital pets to play games, to decorate her pets' living spaces, and to chat with her friends online. She was obsessed with the *Webkinz* world, and the *Webkinz* MMORPG facilitated the blending of real-life play with online play. She was able to see her beloved stuff animals come alive online to talk, run, eat, work, and play.

What happens to our minds when we devote significant hours to a task or an activity? What happens to our brains when we focus hours and hours on a video game? Dr. Robert Stickgold and his research team at Harvard University published an experiment in the research journal *Science* illustrating that people who played the video game *Tetris* for seven hours over a period of three days experienced hallucinatory replay of the activities as they fell asleep.[19] This phenomenon is referred to as "The Tetris Effect". The game *Tetris* is a puzzle game where falling blocks of various shapes must be aligned to form a continuous line.[20] When such a line is created, it disappears, and any block above the deleted line will fall. When a certain number of lines are cleared, the game enters a new level. As the game progresses, each level

19 STICKGOLD ET AL., "REPLAYING THE GAME: HYPNAGOGIC IMAGES IN NORMALS AND AMNESICS." SCIENCE. 2000 OCT 13;290(5490): 350-3.
20 "TETRIS." WIKIPEDIA. HTTP://EN.WIKIPEDIA.ORG/WIKI/TETRIS. ACCESSED SEPTEMBER 19, 2011.

causes the blocks to fall faster. The game ends when the stack of blocks reaches the top of the playing field, and no new blocks are able to fall. Participants playing *Tetris* have reported intrusive visual images of the game at sleep onset.[21]

As gamers become increasingly obsessed with the digital world and invest the majority of their free time playing video games, their minds and sense of reality are continually being molded, skewed, and melded with the digital world. Even when they aren't playing, their minds are likely preoccupied with their chosen game; they're thinking of strategies, how to get their characters' status moved up, what new items to acquire for their characters, or how to further control their empires. When I was away from my computer, my mind never stopped thinking about the games I was addicted to.

During the height of my gluttony for video games, I played more than forty hours a week of *Diablo*, a game where I slayed demonic creatures, undead skeletons, and Diablo, the Devil himself. The game is based on role-playing with a *Dungeons & Dragons* theme, but the action is real-time and attractively animated. When I shot arrows through the undead skeletons, sounds of the bones shattering and hitting the dungeon floor were realistic and contributed to my complete immersion in the demonic world.

21 LEUTWYLER, KRISTIN. "TETRIS DREAMS". SCIENTIFIC AMERICAN. OCTOBER 16, 2000. HTTP://WWW.SCIENTIFICAMERICAN.COM/ARTICLE. CFM?ID=TETRIS-DREAMS. ACCESSED SEPTEMBER 7, 2011.

In *Diablo*, I was the warrior, the rogue, or the sorcerer, hunting and destroying evil. *Diablo* allowed me to connect with other players through Blizzard's Battle.net, and I spent most of my time devoted to playing with other strangers online. I recruited some of my friends to play with me too. I placed more value on my *Diablo* characters than I did on my own real-life relationships.

Once a warrior friend came to my assistance and dropped a rare and very powerful item, a ring called the *Stone of Jordan*. To that point in the game, I have never seen or found the *Stone of Jordan* while killing hundreds, if not thousands, of monsters in the game. It was a highly coveted item and used as currency in the game and could even fetch ten dollars if sold online. When I received this ring from my friend, I was euphoric. I performed the happy dance around my computer, laughing and celebrating. My online friend, someone whom I had never met, had given me a gift I appreciated far more than any tangible gift from a loved one, and this gift was made of nothing but computer code and existed only in the video game *Diablo*.

When my wife and I were struggling in our relationship, we began attending church because we were desperate to rescue our marriage. I was spending too much time online and not investing enough in our relationship. I spoke to my wife very little, and I didn't want to go out on dates. I didn't care what she did with her time. The major purpose in my life was to make my online characters stronger, more powerful, and better equipped. My mind was constantly obsessed with the games. I struggled many times to stay alert during Sunday morning sermons, and often I would fall asleep. As I shifted from falling asleep to being alert, I'd be in a half-awake state and would have vivid dreams about the games.

As I was falling asleep during church one day, I heard loud footsteps on the roof... boom... boom... boom.... Suddenly, Diablo crashed through the ceiling and started to slaughter the congregation. It was the Tetris Effect, only instead of images of falling shapes, I felt as if I was witnessing evil violence. Similar to what I had done a thousand times in the video game *Diablo*, I dreamed of putting on my armor, saving the people gathered to worship, and slaying the Devil. Or should I make an alliance with the Devil and assist him?

Other gamers have reported similar experiences with the melding of the digital world and the physical world. In an article discussing the Tetris Effect, these gamers shared their experiences:[22]

 "After playing a first perspective shooting game

22 EARLING, ANNETTE. "THE TETRIS EFFECT: DO COMPUTER GAMES FRY YOUR BRAIN?" PHILADELPHIA CITYPAPER. MARCH 21–28, 1996. HTTP://ARCHIVES.CITYPAPER.NET/ARTICLES/032196/ARTICLE038. SHTML. ACCESSED SEPTEMBER 11, 2011.

such as Doom or Dark Troopers for a long stretch, for a few days afterwards, I tend to look at the environment around me much the same as in the game—basically, I start at one point, and my goal is to reach another point, no matter where I am going. I map out the floor plan of the best route in my head, even checking off areas I have been before, much like the game itself. And I tend to interact less with the people around me [They ARE the bad guys, after all :)]. "—Tim*

"In my Asteroids playing days, I would find myself reaching for the hyperspace button to escape close calls while driving."—Steve

"When I first started playing Descent, I noticed some interesting carry-overs into the 'real' world. Once, in a supermarket, on the edge of my field of vision, I noticed a bright metallic blue sphere floating in the air (actually a novelty helium balloon) and immediately thought 'Shield powerup!' I had begun to drift toward it before I realized that I wasn't at my computer."—Michael

"I sometimes find that when I do something not the way I should have done it, then I want to do a 'load game'."—Mirko

"You're used to driving 300 mph on the racing game at the mall, then you get in your car and peel out of the mall parking lot like hell on wheels, forgetting where you are."—Michael

In Malcolm Gladwell's book, *Outliers*, he states that 10,000 hours are needed to achieve elite status in any profession, sport, or activity. What does 10,000 hours break down to? Ten thousand hours is full-time work for over four years. Many people are devoting this much time to games, physically as well as mentally, and molding themselves into professional gamers. Yet, reaching the skill level of an elite professional gamer truly means nothing for most gamers. There are, however, a handful of professional video game players who make a living similar to professional athletes, receiving commercial endorsements and prize money.

While most gamers will never generate income from their gaming expertise, many young people are enticed by the possibility, and a common way a person will attempt to rationalize a gaming addiction is by declaring that they intend to become a professional gamer.

While I was speaking to a group of high school students about gaming addiction, a boy raised his hand and argued, "Professional gamers make money." I asked the class if they knew the probability of becoming a professional athlete, a field with many more professionals than gaming. No one did, and the class was shocked to hear that the chances of becoming a professional athlete are about one in 30,000. In professional gaming, there are only a handful of players making over $100,000 annually. The chances are much better for a kid to pursue an education and to become a medical doctor, a profession where there is one doctor for approximately 400 Americans.

Aside from a few career paths such as professional gamers, pilots, or perhaps professional soldiers, few skills translate from the digital world to reality in terms of professional proficiencies or expertise. The problem is that video game addicts cannot moderate their game time, and they waste valuable time playing too much; any real professional expertise gained is wasted, because the gamer cannot function in real life to apply this expertise.

I am not against video games, similar to how I am not against alcohol or casinos. However, I am an advocate for the responsible use of technology and reasonable video game usage. Unfortunately, similar to alcoholics and addictive gamblers, there are people who cannot control their playtime with video games. Children and adults are hooked on video games, social media, and

Internet games without realizing the dangers to their health, lives, and futures.

There are some extremely good uses for video games. For example, they can help educate kids, can improve hand-eye coordination, and can be used to train pilots to fly planes. But there is a point when playing video games becomes excessive and becomes a problem. For example, a pilot who uses a flight simulator to develop flying skills must eventually fly real planes in order to get a real job and make real money. If the pilot is always flying planes in the digital world, he will never be able to attain a real job flying planes.

We make excuses as gamers, claiming that playing games is helping us to develop skills with computers, game design, programming, and professional gaming. Gamers try to meld their real lives with the digital world, justifying the enormous investment of time playing video games. Unfortunately, I have never learned one bit of code while playing a game, and my son has not remembered one bit of history playing *Age of Empires*. I hear from other parents that they allow their kids to play video games because they're interested in "graphic design", or "programming." I then ask what their child's favorite software package is for graphic design or what computer language they know? Most of the time, I get no answer. The truth is that playing games will not teach kids how to design graphics or write computer code, unless the kids can pull themselves away from being hypnotized by the digital world to take computer courses, to study, and to practice.

For many kids and adults, the lure of playing in the digital world is too strong to resist. It is enticingly fun and rewarding for people to be immersed in the world that video games provide. Gaming today has become significantly influential, filled with the power to grip and to invade the minds of even the most intelligent individuals. Gamers experience complete immersion in the digital world. Hundreds of millions of people are hooked on games. And as people become addicted to video games, there inevitably comes a melding of the digital world with reality.

Chapter 12:   The Addiction

Growing up as a Vietnamese immigrant, always trying to fit in while finding my way in life, contributed to my insecurities and bad habits. For one thing, I didn't have direction because I didn't know God. Because my father had bipolar disorder, and it was extremely disruptive, my family unit as a whole was unstable. There were loud and violent arguments in the home. Family members and adult acquaintances were quick to attack me emotionally by calling me stupid or crazy and constantly discounting my ideas. Some of my family's hurtful words were meant to motivate me, but instead they left my heart broken and empty. I had low self-esteem and I felt alone. I could not relate to other people around me. My intense yearning for love and acceptance made me dysfunctional. I would do or say anything to win the approval of others. I was an ideal candidate to embrace addictive behaviors in order to facilitate an escape from emotional pain.

I found strength in leadership classes introduced to me by a junior high teacher, Mr. Fox. I was able to build up my confidence and ego through academics and athletics. But external accolades did not heal insecurities rooted in the soul and heart. As I grew older, unfortunately, I used my confidence and leadership abilities to bully others in order to feel that I had control over something in my life.

Both my father and brother suffer from bipolar disorder. They are what is called rapid cyclers and have manic episodes every year, requiring multiple hospitalizations. One time, my father drove our family in reverse on Highway 26 in Oregon because he was angry with other drivers. He then crashed into a ditch with the entire family in the car. On another occasion, he was determined to raise twenty-five chickens in our suburban neighborhood. The police knew him well because he test-drove new cars and didn't return them to the dealership. I could write an entire book about my dad's adventures. Although some are amusing when retold, these manic escapades were far from amusing to our family at the time and increased my worry that I might have bipolar disorder. Fortunately, I never developed it, but I still didn't feel that I had control of my life. I tore people down to make myself feel better. I verbally berated people publicly if I thought they were weaker than me. I was a mess, emotionally and spiritually. I was lost, angry, hateful, frustrated, and hurt. Above all, I had a deep need for love and acceptance. I was broken, and this behavior carried over into my marriage. I did not know how to be a kind and loving partner. My wife Julie and I argued often and were unable to work as a team. I fell into my old pattern, and I ridiculed and criticized her mercilessly. "You don't do enough around the house." "You're lazy." "You can't even do laundry on time." "Without me you would be nothing."

Coping with marital stress, medical school, the difficulties of graduate school, and raising young children, I dove deeper into Internet video games. In video games, I found respect, acceptance, love, encouragement, challenge, ego boosts, and leadership opportunities. I had control over my video game avatars, toons, and profiles. I selected their physical features and other characteristics. I finally could look the way I envisioned. I felt godly in the games, and I tasted control and power. I enjoyed crushing human opponents, seeing and hearing their anger and profanity while I basked in victory. I loved dominating servers with the guild in *Ultima Online* where we killed and stole from other players. In *Diablo*, I set up situations for other players to die only to hear them beg for mercy and for the return of their hard-earned armor, weapons, and gear. There was nothing good about the way my online friends and I played these games; most of these "friends" I had never met. As an adult, I couldn't bully others in real life without serious consequences, so I turned to games played over the Internet to seek power and control over others. But as I dove deeper into video games, my real life was falling apart.

I remembered what my parents had said during my youth: no drugs, no alcohol, no gambling, and no smoking. But video games were okay; they were my socially acceptable escape mechanism. Video games seemed so benign. How could video games be harmful when they were abundantly available in nearly every store? I grew up with video games, there were ads for them everywhere, and nearly everyone played them. But video games were digital heroin for my mind.

I still functioned okay in real life because I was able to survive on little sleep thanks to the hypomanic traits I had inherited from my father. I went to school and worked in the lab during the day, and then I came home to make dinner, care for my children, and play video games until my wife came home from work. I even volunteered to feed the babies during the middle of the night so my wife could sleep and I could play video games. I perfected bottle-feeding the baby with my left hand, leaving my right hand free to click the mouse and play.

During these wee hours of the night, I gorged my mind on more video games, sometimes playing until four or five in the morning. I slept for a few hours and then repeated the daily cycle. I dreaded hearing the birds chirping because it meant morning had arrived. I was angry with myself for playing all night again. Chronically tired, I often nodded off while driving and would swerve the car onto the shoulder of the road. Other times, I could not recall the last five to ten minutes of the drive. One day, I crashed my car because I was late for my clinical rotation in medical school due to playing *Diablo* that morning. On Sundays, I would sleep nearly all day, recharge, and then on Monday restart my perpetual, never-ending hell all over again. I was a functional addict. I maintained a schedule that would easily have destroyed most people's lives, careers, and futures.

My addiction to video games continued for over nine years, with forty to fifty hours devoted every week to them. Some weeks I played more than fifty hours, particularly during holidays and vacations. I began to change mentally, physically, and spiritually. I was abusive towards my wife and kids, perpetually irritated, and constantly angry. My mind was always preoccupied with video games. I withdrew from my friends and my colleagues, as well as my family. I preferred to be alone so I could sneak in additional hours of play. I was excited when my wife took daily naps with the kids because it meant more game time for me. I loved it when my wife went to bed early, which meant more hours to play before I heard the chirping birds in the morning.

But playing at home was not enough. I used computer boot disks so I could play *Warcraft II* with other people using *Kali* in the medical library between lectures and during lunch. I had bouts of rage when I lost matches. I yelled profanity at my computer screen and slammed down my mouse. I pounded the keyboard. I was furious with my wife for asking me to take gaming breaks, to be away from the only thing that made me feel good and gave me an escape from life. I blamed her for being insecure, needy, and demanding of my time. I blamed everyone else for my insecurities.

Increasingly, I needed my video game fix in large amounts of time; otherwise, I was irritable and angry. I was depressed when I wasn't playing. I had become spiritually empty, and I had very little self-esteem. I felt ashamed that I played so much, but I couldn't stop playing. My need for challenges, my hunger for ego, my thirsty mind, and my lonely soul required that I deliver small, quick bursts of dopamine into my mind to keep me on that high. I was the rat in the Skinner box. I knew my lever was the keyboard and mouse. My rewards were the euphoric experiences video games offered.

With excessive play, I even began manifesting physical symptoms. I stopped exercising and lifting weights. I had frequent headaches, chronic red and dry eyes, and stretch marks from my rapid thirty-pound weight gain. I had urinary incontinence problems and hemorrhoids because of the extreme amount of time that I spent sitting, playing ladder matches and tournaments online, neglecting my body's needs and not using the bathroom. I was constantly uploading junk into my mind, and my body was malfunctioning.

Eventually I crushed my wife's spirit with a constant barrage of severe verbal abuse. It got to the point that she was afraid for herself and for the kids. I broke chairs, punched walls, and threw items around the house, yelling: "I hate you!", "You're holding me back!", "Why are you so needy?", and "Stop crying—you're so weak." At one point, she was rocking back and forth in a fetal position, in disbelief that she had married a monster, a zombie who couldn't unplug from the digital world. When it became unbearable for her, she secretly moved three thousand miles away with the help of her mother. She filed a restraining order against me and petitioned for divorce and custody of the kids. These events completely devastated me. She was my last connection to the real world. I had played so many hours and so many years that I hadn't maintained relationships with real friends and family members. During the height of my video game addiction, I had stopped calling my family or hanging out with friends. I was an agnostic with no faith and no guidance whatsoever. And yet, I remember one day lying on the floor crying, praying to any god that would listen to me. I prayed for help and for the return of my family.

I began contemplating and planning my suicide. I had only two years remaining in the eight years required for my MD-PhD degree at one of the most prestigious medical schools in the world. To outsiders, it appeared that I had everything. But in truth, I had lost all of my friends, my wife, and my kids. My soul was empty. I had nothing. My mother immediately flew out to live with me. Her intervention and loving presence truly saved my life. Eventually, after $20,000 spent on divorce attorneys and custody battles for the kids, my wife gave me a second chance but only with the understanding that I would start going to church with her. Out of desperation, I agreed, but I still would not acknowledge that my video game addiction was a problem. I blamed my past wounds and stresses for my spiraling out of control.

I tried playing video games less often after my wife moved back, but I couldn't play video games in moderation. I had started an Internet business on eBay during medical school, which helped to distract me from video games for a short while. I was replacing the dopamine rush I felt with video games with the gambling rush of selling items on eBay for profit. I sold Pokémon cards, items around the house, electronics, and even a broken microscope. I started all my auctions at a penny-starting bid and let the auctions go, anticipating the final bids similar to a gambler waiting for the payout. Pokémon cards that I purchased for $10 sold for over $50. A broken microscope that was junk, acquired for free from a lab throwing it away, sold for over $600. I made enough income from the business for my wife to quit her job as a nurse, but I only had to devote two hours a day to maintaining my business. Because I was providing for the family and surviving medical school, I justified spending my free time playing video games to help me relax and to escape from the daily grind. As a result of all the years of playing games, I had rewired my brain to desire the digital heroin that video games offered.

Consequently, I adopted old habits again and invested more time in video games. My devotion to my wife and family faded again. There were many nights when my wife went to bed and waited for me to join her after I had finished playing games, only to fall asleep alone. I lost interest in sex and all that really mattered. I didn't even want to spend Christmas with the family. I encouraged my wife and kids to spend Christmas with my wife's parents while I stayed behind during my only week off during my internal medicine internship. That week I logged over 250 games on *Starcraft*, amounting to over 100 hours. After that week, I played when the family was asleep or was busy doing other things, such as going to the park or movies or school functions. My daughter recognized my addiction to video games when she was only five years old. She drew a picture with the following caption, "This is Mom, Brother, Dog, and me at the park.

This is Daddy, fat, and sad because he doesn't go to the park and only plays games."

   I developed carpal tunnel syndrome in my right forearm and right index finger during my ophthalmology residency; this was because of the excessive mouse clicking I did while playing real-time strategy games. Carpal tunnel syndrome is inflammation of the tissues in the wrist and forearm caused by repetitive motions, and the excruciating pain in my forearm was hindering me from performing eye surgery. I had to take maximum doses of anti-inflammatory medications in order to function as a physician and to write in the medical charts. Intraocular eye surgery requires fine movements of the fingers and wrist. The ocular space that eye surgeons work in is about eight millimeters wide by five millimeters deep. Moving surgical instruments beyond this space can cause complications for the patient, including blindness. With carpal tunnel syndrome in my dominant arm, I was not able to move instruments in the eye without pain, and the pain was causing me to have tremors during surgery. My carpal tunnel syndrome finally woke me up. I realized that excessive video game playing was harming my health and that my addictive behavior was destroying me. Because I was hooked on games, I risked my life, my marriage, and, now, my medical career. My medical career is what I had worked so hard for, my way out of poverty as an immigrant. I considered it my biggest accolade.

At about this time, as a part of my agreement with my wife when she moved back in with me, I participated in a Bible study with her. Originally, I attended the study out of duty, but little did I know it would be the event that would lead me to a fork in the road of my life. We read the *Purpose Driven Life* by Rick Warren, and I discovered that I was created with a specific purpose. I saw that I could use my gifts for this purpose, or I could continue to waste them. I chose the path of purpose, and I found the love and acceptance I had been seeking my entire life. Finally, after over a decade of struggling and almost losing everything that mattered in my life, I found my way through God's guidance and discovered the path to recovery. I did not try to moderate my playing. I did not cut back. By God's grace, I stopped playing completely.

However, even after three years of not playing any video games, I still felt urges to play. Addiction is a life-long battle; once an addict, always an addict.

The brain releases a neurotransmitter called dopamine when a person experiences rewarding situations, particularly in behavioral addictions such as eating disorders, sex addiction, gambling addiction and video game addiction. Dopamine is also associated with drug and alcohol abuse.[23] As the rewarding experiences contin-

23 NATIONAL INSTITUTE OF DRUG ABUSE. "NIDA INFOFACTS: UNDERSTANDING DRUG ABUSE AND ADDICTION." HTTP://WWW.NIDA. NIH.GOV/INFOFACTS/UNDERSTAND.HTML. ACCESSED SEPTEMBER 4, 2011.

ue, the neuronal connections and memory connections associated with the euphoric experiences are strengthened and remodel the connections in the brain. When a video game addict stops gaming, the brain loses the stimuli that release the same rewarding highs associated with the dopamine rush. The brain also adapts to the high levels of dopamine by developing what is known as tolerance. The brain produces less dopamine and/or reduces the number of dopamine receptors in the reward circuit, which decreases the enjoyment of the drugs and addictive behavior, requiring the addict to increase the drug or behavior to have any good feelings. Otherwise, the video game addict can suffer from depression and physical withdrawal when they stop playing games.

Data presented at the British Psychological Society conference in Dublin showed that video game addicts missed meals and went without sleep to spend more time playing. They suffered withdrawal symptoms and had difficulties cutting back. Additionally, they were found to be more introverted, emotionally unstable, and had lower self-esteem than the average person.[24] Presumably, addicts' brains have built up the ability to produce and release dopamine associated with addictive behaviors. There is growing research evidence that

---

24 FLEMING, NIC. "VIDEO GAME ADDICTION 'LIKE BEING ON DRUGS.'" THE TELEGRAPH. APRIL 3, 2008. HTTP://WWW.TELEGRAPH.CO.UK/ EARTH/EARTHNEWS/3338422/VIDEO-GAME-ADDICTION-LIKE-BEING-ON-DRUGS.HTML. ACCESSED SEPTEMBER 2, 2011.

dopamine is released with video game play.[25, 26]

The link between dopamine and video game play has been published in the scientific journal *Nature* and the *Journal of Addiction Medicine*. While doing research for this book, I was looking at screen shots of new games and MMORPGs. The screen shots made me feel the urge to play these games. After looking at images of the games and recalling gaming scenarios that excited me, I experienced the shakes for twelve hours. I took my temperature and it was normal, but my scalp hurt, my back tingled with pins and needles, and I had bouts of nausea. The next day, I was depressed and I had no energy. I was having withdrawal symptoms from only seeing these still images of the games.

According to the American Society of Addiction Medicine, "Addiction is a primary, chronic disease of brain reward, motivation, memory and related circuitry. Dysfunction in these circuits leads to characteristic biological, psychological, social and spiritual manifestations. This is reflected in an individual pathologically pursuing reward and/or relief by substance use and other behaviors. Addiction is characterized by inability to consistently abstain, impairment in behavioral control, craving,

25 KOEPP ET AL. "EVIDENCE FOR STRIATAL DOPAMINE RELEASE DURING A VIDEO GAME." NATURE. 1998 MAY 21; 393(6682): 266—8.
26 HAN ET AL. "DOPAMINE GENES AND REWARD DEPENDENCE IN ADOLESCENTS WITH EXCESSIVE INTERNET VIDEO GAME PLAY." J ADDICT MED. 2007 SEP; 1(3): 133—8.

diminished recognition of significant problems with one's behaviors and interpersonal relationships, and a dysfunctional emotional response. Like other chronic diseases, addiction often involves cycles of relapse and remission. Without treatment or engagement in recovery activities, addiction is progressive and can result in disability or premature death."[27]

Video game addiction is not yet an official medical diagnosis. However, a leading council of the nation's largest group of doctors supports the fact that video game addiction should be included in the widely used mental illness manual created and published by the American Psychiatric Association, the *Diagnostic and Statistical Manual of Mental Disorders*.[28] Video game companies reject the notion that their products can cause a psychiatric illness, and this issue generates much debate. The next issue of the *Diagnostic and Statistical Manual of Mental Disorders* will be finished after the writing of this book, and it is unclear whether or not the American Psychiatric Association will list video game addiction as an official diagnosis. On the other hand, game designers have a monetary incentive to make video games addictive in the more than $25 billion and growing video

27 *AMERICAN SOCIETY OF ADDICTION MEDICINE. HTTP://WWW.ASAM. ORG/ABOUT.HTML. ACCESSED AUGUST 31, 2011.*
28 *HEALTHWATCH. "VIDEO GAME ADDICTION: A MEDICAL DISORDER?" CBS NEWS. JANUARY 18, 2011. HTTP://WWW.CBSNEWS. COM/STORIES/2007/06/21/HEALTH/MAIN2965003.SHTML. ACCESSED SEPTEMBER 1, 2011.*

game industry.

For millions of video game addicts, including myself, video game addiction is real and has horrendous
health and mental consequences. Video game addiction is digital heroin for the mind that makes the gamer
feel good, but also helps them to escape from reality.
The addict pushes buttons and enters commands on a
keyboard to receive video, audio, and tactile stimuli.
These stimuli are sent to the brain where memories are
formed and associated with the behavior and the emotional and physical responses to it. When memories are
formed, the brain expresses gene transcription factors
that control the expression of proteins and receptors
regulating brain function. [29] When an action, tied to a
reward, is reinforced over and over again, the brain is
rewired through gene expression. [30] The memories, the
behavior, and the neurochemical responses of the brain
are associated together, and the behavioral addiction is
strengthened over time.

An article published by *Scientific American* showed
that Internet addiction, especially online gaming, re-
wires structures in the brain. It also goes on to explain

29 KUBIK S, MIYASHITA T, GUZOWSKI JF. "USING IMMEDIATE EARLY
GENES TO MAP HIPPOCAMPAL SUBREGIONAL FUNCTIONS." LEARN
MEMORY. 2007 NOV 14; 14(11): 758—70. PRINT 2007 NOV.
30 BLUM ET AL. "REWARD CIRCUITRY DOPAMINERGIC ACTIVATION
REGULATES FOOD AND DRUG CRAVING BEHAVIOR." CURR PHARM DES.
2011; 17(12): 1158—67.

that surface-level brain matter shrinks the longer the gamer is an addict. The author explains that this shrinkage could lead to negative effects such as reduced inhibition of inappropriate behaviors and diminished goal orientation.[31]

Video game addiction is an insidious and growing problem around the world. While not all individuals develop an addiction when playing video games, gamers who become addicts are likely to have biological and genetic factors, environmental influences, and developmental elements that contribute to their addictive behavior. A study in the journal *Pediatrics* by Dr. Gentile reports that the prevalence of pathological video gaming is similar around the world, with approximately nine percent of youths demonstrating addictive behavior. Greater amounts of time playing video games, lower social competence, and greater impulsivity seemed to act as risk factors for becoming pathological gamers. Depression, anxiety, social phobias, and lower school performance are often outcomes of pathological gaming.[32]

Video game access is widespread, with nearly every

31 MOSHER, DAVE. "HIGH WIRED: DOES ADDICTIVE INTERNET USE RESTRUCTURE THE BRAIN?" SCIENTIFIC AMERICAN. JUNE 17, 2011. HTTP://WWW.SCIENTIFICAMERICAN.COM/ARTICLE.CFM?ID=DOES-ADDICTIVE-INTERNET-USE-RESTRUCTURE-BRAIN. ACCESSED AUGUST 31, 2011.
32 GENTILE ET AL., "PATHOLOGICAL VIDEO GAME USE AMONG YOUTHS: A TWO-YEAR LONGITUDINAL STUDY." PEDIATRICS. 2011 FEB;127(2):E319-29. EPUB 2011 JAN 17.

home owning or having access to video games. If you have Facebook, then you have access to social media games. If you have the Internet, you have access to games. Children of all socioeconomic classes are affected. Often, I observe kids in public glued to their portable gaming devices with zombie-like eyes, oblivious of their surroundings. Kids can become video game addicts because parents are feeding the addiction, using the video games as digital pacifiers. Although most parents do not provide access to alcohol or drugs for their children, nine in ten American homes provide video games with unregulated time for play and lack of education on the proper use of the technology. Many parents do not know the signs and symptoms of video game addiction so they do not know to intervene.

Let's consider Luke. One of my good friends invited a surgeon friend and his teenage son, Luke, to his home for dinner and a swim. The first thing that Luke asked was if there were any video games in the house. My friend said there might be an old video game console in storage. Luke begged him to set up the console. After spending hours trying to set up the old video game console, my friend was unsuccessful in connecting it to his new LCD television. The child was so fixated on finding video games to play that he was unable to socialize and to enjoy the pool. He was seeking video games like a junkie who needed a quick fix. Luke comes from a highly educated family of physicians. Even highly educated families can be unaware of video game addiction and its serious physical and mental manifestations.

I want to make it clear that I am not against video games. I am, however, an advocate for responsible video game playing. And just as there are some adults who can have an occasional alcoholic beverage without losing control and becoming an alcoholic, it is certainly possible for people to play video games without becoming addicts. I believe, however, that if more people are educated on the potential physical, mental, and emotional dangers associated with excessive video game use, then we have a chance to prevent hundreds of millions of youths worldwide from falling into a perpetual digital hell. Young people hear about the dangerous possibility of alcoholism or gambling addiction, but our society still underestimates how powerful and rampant gaming addiction is today. In a recent interview, Kevin Roberts, author of *Cyber Junkie: Escape the Gaming and Internet Trap*, who works with kids addicted to video games, shared that, "There is a growing problem with video game addiction in the eighteen to twenty-nine year-old age group. This group of gamers were restricted [video game time] when living with parents but are out of control once on their own."[33] Although there are no accurate estimates on the cost to society, the lost in productivity is enormous because millions of individuals

33 HTTP://KEVINJROBERTS.NET/

will not be able to contribute to their communities but instead will become a drain on resources.

I have found that moderation is the key to a rewarding and happy life. Too much of anything can be harmful. Let's consider something we all need: water. In 2007, there was a contest in California with the theme "Hold Your Wee for a Wii," where contestants drank a large amount of water in hopes of winning a Nintendo Wii. This promotional stunt resulted in the death of Jennifer Strange after she drank so much water that she diluted the sodium chloride (salt) concentration in her blood.[34] Sodium chloride concentration is important for normal nerve conduction as well as regulating the flow of water in and out of the cells via osmosis. When the salt concentration in the blood becomes too diluted, one of the first things that occurs is brain swelling, which can lead to death.

This tragedy illustrates that even water is dangerous in large amounts. Similarly, video games in large amounts are harmful. In the ideal world, it would be great if we all could play video games for less than one hour daily. Unfortunately, for many gamers, moderation is not possible because the games are designed to entice people and to keep them playing by providing a sense of achieve-

---

34 BBC NEWS. "WHY IS TOO MUCH WATER DANGEROUS?" BBC. JANUARY 15, 2007. HTTP://NEWS.BBC.CO.UK/2/HI/UK_NEWS/MAGAZINE/6263029. STM. ACCESSED SEPTEMBER 2, 2011.

ment, social interaction, and total immersion.[35] Highly successful games entice tens of millions of gamers to sit for hours clicking the mouse, reinforcing behaviors, and releasing dopamine in the brain. Likewise, the video game addict is excited when seeing a gaming computer, keyboard, mouse, and video game images. Not everyone who plays video games will be an addict. However, if gamers cannot moderate play, then complete abstinence is necessary to break the addictive behavior.

Video game addiction is insidious, like a chronic disease where the mind slowly zones out to reality. The addict stops caring for activities of daily living: bills are missed, relationships are neglected, exercise is forgotten, meetings are missed, sick days are increased, jobs are lost, sleep is decreased, school performance is poor, and hobbies are neglected. By the time the individual realizes that video game addiction is a problem, the gamer barely resembles the person who first started playing. The video game addict is emotionally, spiritually, and physically ill. If video game addiction is not recognized for the disease it really is, more people will experience lost opportunities, ruined relationships, and even death in extreme cases. Video game addiction is very real, and the sooner we recognize this, the sooner we can slow its rapid growth.

---

35 YEE N. "MOTIVATIONS FOR PLAY IN ONLINE GAMES." CYBERPSYCHOL BEHAV 2006; 9: 772–775.

Chapter 13: Not Alone

Rehabgamer, the online alias of an adult video game addict in his fifties, imagines a recipe for the perfect recreational drug. It is not designed for anyone else but you. Your needs, wants, and desires all rolled into one and in just the right amounts.

1) Two cups of escape from reality to not think about life's problems or issues.

2) One cup finely chopped rewards to stimulate the pleasure centers. Add a dash of positive feedback from other players to enhance the effect if desired.

3) Eight ounces of whole organic fantasy to be the person you want to be. Don't forget to personalize the avatar to increase your identity with your online persona.

4) Two ounces of stimulation and challenge to become totally engaged in the activity and to make sure you lose all track of time.

5)   Three ready-to-go social groups to build friends and relationships that may be lacking. Make sure you develop deep bonds with these groups that transcend any you have in real life.

6)   Add a sense of accomplishment to taste. This will add to the euphoria and ensure satisfaction.

7)   A pinch of "pwning noobs" [i.e., dominating and killing new players in the game] to feel powerful.

Combine all of the ingredients in a virtual bowl and mix. Make sure they are well blended to balance out the desired taste. Then bake slowly. You don't want to cook it too quickly or it may burn and then you will have to create a new drug. Also, note it is best to just leave it in the oven on low so you can get a warm taste whenever you want. It is never really done, and the more you cook it the better it tastes.

The following stories of video game addiction are real and depict how gaming addicts have created their own recipes for the perfect recreational drug and allowed them to destroy their lives.

MAN JAILED FOR PLANE TETRIS GAME

Faiz Chopdat was returning from Luxor in Egypt to Manchester Airport in England when he was seen with his mobile phone switched on.[36] He was playing the popular game *Tetris* after he had been warned twice by cabin staff and once by a passenger to switch off the phone, which triggered an argument during the Air 2000 flight. Chopdat's obsession to play *Tetris* resulted in a guilty verdict by a jury for endangering the safety of an aircraft. Chopdat was jailed for four months.

Even such a simple game as *Tetris* involves the risk and reward system that players find so addictive. It seems likely that, if asked, the man in this story would not say that four months in jail was worth the high score he got by fighting to continue his game; but on that plane, in the grip of addiction, nothing mattered more to him than the game.

---

36 CNN. "MAN JAILED FOR PLAYAING TETRIS GAME." CNN WORLD. SEPTEMBER 11, 2002. HTTP://EDITION.CNN.COM/2002/WORLD/ EUROPE/09/10/UK.PLANE.MOBILE/. ACCESSED SEPTEMBER 11, 2011.

PRISONERS FORCED TO FARM FOR GOLD

In the game *World of Warcraft*, gamers need virtual gold to play. Virtual gold allows the players to upgrade their gear (armor and weapons), advance their skills, and acquire new skills in the video game. Farming for gold is the act of earning virtual gold in the game, taking literally hours and hours of playing in order to build up enough gold to be successful and may require a time investment equivalent to having a second job. When I first played *World of Warcraft*, I did not see my first gold piece in the game until two months after I started playing. I became frustrated with the significant time commitment needed to acquire gold. I found an online source for *World of Warcraft* gold that offered $100 for 100 *World of Warcraft* gold pieces. I paid the $100, and within 24 hours I received the virtual gold pieces in my account from another player on the server. The demand for virtual goods, items that only exist in video games, was estimated to be between $300 million and $400 million annually in 2007.[37]

A 2011 *Guardian News* article illustrates the high demand for virtual *World of Warcraft* gold and how lucrative gold farming can be, where prisoners were forced to play games for hours at a time, until prisoners could

---

37 JIMENEZ, CRISTINA. "THE HIGH COST OF PLAYING WARCRAFT." HTTP://NEWS.BBC.CO.UK/2/HI/TECHNOLOGY/7007026.STM. BBC NEWS. ACCESSED SEPTEMBER 4, 2011.

barely see straight.[38] Nearly three hundred prisoners in China performed physical labor by day and at night were forced to play *World of Warcraft* to farm virtual gold. If the prisoners did not meet their quotas, they were brutally beaten with plastic pipes.

ADDICTION TO SOCIAL MEDIA

Cynthia was addicted to Facebook.[39] When her twelve-year-old daughter asked her for help with her homework, Cynthia said she was too busy on Facebook to help. So her daughter went upstairs to her room and sent a Facebook message asking her for help. Cynthia said, "I'm an addict. I just get lost in Facebook. My daughter gets so PO'd at me, and really it is kind of pathetic. It's not something I'm particularly proud of. I just get so sucked in."

Cynthia spent about twenty hours a week on the social networking website. She tried to cut down on her Facebook use but failed. Although there are no statistics

38 VINCENT, DANNY. "CHINA USED PRISONERS IN LUCRATIVE INTERNET GAMING WORK." GUARDIAN NEWS. MAY 25, 2011. HTTP:// WWW.GUARDIAN.CO.UK/WORLD/2011/MAY/25/CHINA-PRISONERS-INTERNET-GAMING-SCAM. ACCESSED SEPTEMBER 4, 2011.
39 COHEN, ELIZABETH. "FIVE CLUES THAT YOU ARE ADDICTED TO FACEBOOK." CNN HEALTH. APRIL 23, 2009. HTTP://ARTICLES.CNN. COM/2009-04-23/HEALTH/EP.FACEBOOK.ADDICT_1_FACEBOOK-PAGE-FACEBOOK-WORLD-SOCIAL-NETWORKING?_S=PM:HEALTH. ACCESSED SEPTEMBER 4, 2011.

on "Facebook addiction," therapists are seeing more people like Cynthia who've crossed the line from social networking to social dysfunction. Paula Pile, a marriage and family therapist in Greensboro, North Carolina, said, "Last Friday, I had three clients in my office with Facebook problems. It's turned into a compulsion—a compulsion to dissociate from your real world and go live in the Facebook world."

I think the addiction to social media relies on the concept of quantity of social interactions versus quality of social interactions. As stated before, nearly 40 percent of men and 53 percent of women who play online games said their virtual friends were equal to or better than their real-life friends, according to a survey of 30,000 gamers.[40] It is clear that online interactions have value for people, but the quality of the online interaction is not as valuable as face-to-face encounters. Also, it is easier to look better on a web page than it is in real life. People present their best characteristics and photos. The interactions on social media websites do not generate the same emotional value as real-life interactions, but it is easier to socially interact on a website than it is face-to-face. Unfortunately, for some people, social media generates enough of a feel-good factor that they invest more time online than in real-life relationships.

40 ALTER, ALEXANDRA. "IS THIS MAN CHEATING ON HIS WIFE?" WALL STREET JOURNAL. AUGUST 10, 2007. HTTP://ONLINE.WSJ.COM/ARTICLE/SB118670164592393622.HTML. ACCESSED AUGUST 27, 2011.

RAPE AND MURDER

Two teenage boys who played numerous hours in the game *World of Warcraft* planned and carried out a brutal murder of an innocent eighteen-year-old girl. After luring her to an empty home, they sexually assaulted her and killed her; then they dragged her body into the woods and set it on fire. After the murder, they bragged about it to other *World of Warcraft* gamers. One of the teenagers admitted that it didn't "feel" the way he thought it would, while the other teenager involved said he'd dreamt of killing someone since he was a boy.[41]

According to Dr. Bonnie Leadbeater, a psychology professor at the University of Victoria, some kids have trouble knowing that what's acceptable in a game may not be okay in real life. Dr. Leadbeater said, "You don't know which aggressive kid is going to take the fantasies of video games and try them out in reality. You just can't predict those very rare occurrences. There would have been signs early. I don't know these two boys at all, but, generally, kids who go on to kill other kids or to act out in this sort of extreme manner are having problems early."

The research is inconclusive as to whether or not violent video games elicit violent tendencies in gamers.

41 MARTINEZ, EDECIO. "WORLD OF WARCRAFT PLAYED ROLE IN RAPE, MURDER OF CANADIAN GIRL KIMBERLY PROCTOR, EXPERTS SAY." CBS NEWS. OCTOBER 29, 2010. HTTP://WWW.CBSNEWS.COM/8301-504083_162-20021194-504083.IITML. ACCESSED SEPTEMBER 4, 2011.

However, this story is of interest because gamers who become obsessed with or addicted to video games can meld their virtual gaming world with reality. Could video game addiction facilitate the manifestation of hidden violent tendencies in people? Dr. Gentile states, "As you might expect, not every study shows exactly the same results, but when we look at the studies overall, the preponderance of evidence suggests that people who play violent video games become more desensitized to violence, have more aggressive feelings, more aggressive thoughts, and are more willing to behave aggressively—especially when provoked. Exposure to aggressive video game content also reduces cooperative, pro-social behaviors."[42]

42 GENTILE, D. "EDITORIAL: PROS/CONS: SCHWARZENEGGER V. EMA." GAMEPRO. OCTOBER 8, 2010. HTTP://WWW.GAMEPRO.COM/ARTICLE/ NEWS/216849/EDITORIAL-PROS-CONS-SCHWARZENEGGER-V-EMA/ ACCESSED SEPTEMBER 7, 2011.

MOTHER NEGLECTS AND KILLS THREE-YEAR-OLD DAUGHTER WHILE PLAYING WORLD OF WARCRAFT

Rebecca Christie, who denied her three-year-old daughter food and drink, was sentenced to twenty-five years in prison after her neglect led to the child's starvation and death.[43] The mother was attached to her computer for excessive periods of time playing *World of Warcraft*, sometimes playing more than fifteen hours straight. Rebecca neglected her child while she played online, resulting in her daughter's gradual starvation and death. The house had an overflowing litter box and a pervasive smell of cat urine. The child ate cat food because there was little food in the house. Rebecca Christie's hands, which once spent hours clicking the mouse to play online games, must now bear the blood of her little girl.

This sad story illustrates the grim reality of video game addiction. For the video game addict, the only thing that matters is the digital world. The digital world is the video game addict's highest priority and the source of their personal identity. Everything in the real world matters little.

---

43 ASSOCIATED PRESS. "NEW MEXICO MOM GETS 25 YEARS FOR STARVING DAUGHTER." FOX NEWS. JUNE 3, 2011. HTTP://WWW. FOXNEWS.COM/US/2011/06/03/NEW-MEXICO-MOM-GETS-25-YEARS-FOR-STARVING-DAUGHTER/. ACCESSED SEPTEMBER 4, 2011.

MURDER OVER A VIRTUAL SWORD

The game *Legend of Mir* is a popular online MMORPG that features a variety of heroes and villains that use magical swords. The game claimed to have 120 million players worldwide at one point. When Shanghai online game player Qiu Chengwei found out that his competitor Zhu Caoyuan stole his virtual dragon sabre, he went to the police and tried to report the theft of the virtual sword, but the police did not take action. Qiu decided to take action himself. He went to Zhu's home and stabbed him repeatedly, killing him to defend a sword that only existed in the digital world. It's becoming more common to see online gamers, in games like *Second Life*, trying to seek justice through real-life court systems over stolen virtual weapons and property.[44]

Similar to when I received my first *Stone of Jordan* in the game *Diablo*, I placed great value on a virtual item. Video games that offer rare game items share commonalities with games of chance and gambling. Gamers place enormous value on magical or rare virtual items, sometimes paying hundreds of dollars for one item. In the story of Qiu, his magical sword was extremely valuable and may have required countless hours to acquire.

44 FINLAYSON, AMALIE. "ONLINE GAMER KILLED FOR SELLING VIRTUAL WEAPON." SYDNEY MORNING HERALD. MARCH 30, 2005. HTTP://WWW.SMH.COM.AU/NEWS/WORLD/ONLINE-GAMER-KILLED-FOR-SELLING-VIRTUAL-WEAPON/2005/03/30/1111862440188.HTML. ACCESSED SEPTEMBER 4, 2011.

For a video game addict, whether it is a *Stone of Jordan* or a magical sword, loss of a highly valued virtual item elicits intense frustration, sadness, and anger. The video game addict places great value on things that exist only in the digital world.

MURDER OVER XBOX

Seventeen-year-old Daniel Petric was convicted of shooting his parents in the head after they took away his Xbox and *Halo 3* game.[45] Daniel killed his mother and wounded his father when they banned him from playing the video game. Judge James Burge convicted him of aggravated murder for the death of his mother and attempted aggravated murder for the attack on his father. On the night of the crime, Daniel took back the video game and used his father's 9-mm handgun to commit the murder. His father testified that his son came into the room and asked, "Would you guys close your eyes? I have a surprise for you." He had expected a pleasant surprise, but then his head went numb from the gunshot. The teenager put the gun in his father's hand in an attempt to make the shootings look like a

45 HARVEY, MIKE. "TEENAGER DANIEL PETRIC SHOT PARENTS WHO TOOK AWAY XBOX." THE TIMES. JANUARY 13, 2009. HTTP://WWW. TIMESONLINE.CO.UK/TOL/NEWS/WORLD/US_AND_AMERICAS/ ARTICLE5512446.ECE. ACCESSED SEPTEMBER 11, 2011.

murder-suicide. When he fled the scene, he took only one item with him: the *Halo 3* video game.

This boy was so possessed by his desire for this game that he did the unthinkable in order to continue to play. Like a cocaine junkie, video game addicts will do things to keep playing that they would never do in their right minds. This story is an extreme case, but it is common for addicts to pretend to be sick so they can skip work, lie to loved ones to get out of commitments, and many other uncharacteristic behaviors, all so they can keep their digital drug flowing.

SOUTH KOREAN MAN DIES AFTER GAMING SESSION

A twenty-eight-year-old Korean man collapsed after playing fifty hours of the game *Starcraft*. He had recently been fired from his job because he was missing work in order to play games. After his lengthy gaming binge, he was physically exhausted, had not eaten properly, and had not taken adequate breaks from the game. When his gaming session ended, he passed out and was taken to the hospital, where he later died. It was presumed that his death was caused by heart failure due to exhaustion.[46]

---

46 ONE-MINUTE WORLD NEWS. "S. KOREAN DIES AFTER GAMES SESSION." BBC NEWS. AUGUST 10, 2005. HTTP://NEWS.BBC.CO.UK/2/

In previous chapters, evidence was provided linking video game playing to the release of dopamine in the brain. Dopamine is an important feel-good neurotransmitter. With too little dopamine, people are depressed. Dopamine makes people feel euphoric, happy, and content. When we play video games, our brains are receiving bursts of dopamine, and we feel good and happy. We don't feel hungry and we don't feel tired while playing video games, as long as the dopamine levels are flowing in the brain. The death of this Korean man illustrates an extreme case of video game addiction where a person forgot basic nutrition while playing.

SUICIDE AFTER PLAYING WORLD OF WARCRAFT

A boy obsessed with the *World of Warcraft* killed himself by jumping out of a twenty-four-story window. After reading letters and a handwritten note, his parents believed he thought he could meet his favorite Warcraft Night Elf hero if he reenacted a scene from the game.[47] The Tetris Effect describes the melding of virtual worlds with reality. Could obsessive and excessive video game

HI/TECHNOLOGY/4137782.3TM. ACCESSED SEPTEMBER 4, 2011.
47 CHEUNG, HUMPHREY. "PARENTS BLAME DEATH OF SON ON WORLD OF WARCRAFT." TG DAILY. NOVEMBER 22, 2005. HTTP://WWW.TGDAILY.COM/BUSINESS-AND-LAW-FEATURES/21757-PARENTS-BLAME-DEATH-OF-SON-ON-WORLD-OF-WARCRAFT.
ACCESSED SEPTEMBER 4, 2011.

play warp the minds of gamers to the point that severely addicted players are unable to distinguish between right and wrong?

The story of Shawn Woolley killing himself for game-related reasons was not an isolated event. This is a new addiction for a new generation, and many parents are bewildered by their children's obsession. They find it difficult to come to grips with the existence and severity of this kind of addiction. Many parents have been educated that addictions to things such as drugs, alcohol, and dieting can lead to severe depression and even suicidal tendencies; but because of the lack of information about video game addiction, many parents don't realize the severe emotional toll video games can take, and they don't step in until it is too late and addiction has taken hold.

XBOX DEATH

A twenty-year-old man died of a deep vein thrombosis (DVT), a condition that is prompted by long periods of sitting, after playing Xbox for twelve hours or more. Usually, DVT is a disease affecting the elderly with sedentary life styles. This health problem is extremely rare in twenty-year-olds. The man's father explains that his son lived for his Xbox and that he played for hours on end. After playing for an extended period of time and complaining of chest pain, the young man collapsed, and medical professionals were unable to save him. He suffered from a pulmonary embolism, where a blood clot in the leg traveled through a vein and into the lungs—a fatal and tragic ending to a twenty-year-old's life.[48] In addition to emotional ramifications, excessive video game play may lead to severe physical and health consequences.

This young man's father says he lived for his Xbox. Ultimately, he died for it. Was the satisfaction he got from playing games worth giving his life? Certainly it was not. But every day young people all over the world are giving days, months, even years of their precious lives in exchange for the thrill the games give them.

In isolation, these stories sound bizarre, and many people don't believe that addiction to video games is a factor. But video game addiction is very real. When these stories are read collectively, it's evident that video game addiction can provide serious heartache, tragedy, and loss, and these are only a fraction of the stories out there. I could include page after page of similar accounts.

The severity of the addiction varies greatly from per-

48 LITTLE, EMMA. "XBOX TRAGEDY." THE SUN. JULY 30, 2011. HTTP://WWW.THESUN.CO.UK/SOL/HOMEPAGE/NEWS/3723107/LAD-OF-20-IS-KILLED-BY-BLOOD-CLOT-CAUSED-BY-PLAYING-HIS-XBOX-FOR-UP-TO-12-HOURS-AT-A-TIME.HTML. ACCESSED SEPTEMBER 5, 2011.

son to person, and so do the consequences. The stories in this chapter are examples of severe addiction, resulting in violence and death. The signs of mild addiction might be subtler, such as rapid weight gain, depression, and loss of ambition, but they are damaging none-the-less. Even though video game addiction is not yet a medical diagnosis, it does not mean the addiction is not real. Many video games share similarities with gambling behavior. Pathologic gambling is considered a medical condition, with a clinical diagnostic code, related to lack of impulse control where the individual seeks the dopamine highs of gambling regardless of the social, personal and financial ramifications of the addictive gambling behavior. In the U.S., there are clinical programs to treat addictive gambling behavior. Many video games utilize gambling strategies to reward gamers, for instance, kill boss and receive a random drop. These random drops can be rare items that have real monetary value, sometimes thousands of dollars. Gamers place incredible worth on rare drops in the game as it requires extensive time to acquire these rare items. If video game design is similar to games of chance seen in casinos, then would it not make sense that certain individuals can develop impulse disorders with video games, similar to people who become addicted to gambling? I am speaking from personal experience of selling and buying virtual items from games like *Diablo* on eBay. My *Windforce* bow was worth about $200 on eBay and when I saw the drop, the excitement and rush from seeing the legendary bow drop after killing the boss was intense and incredible!

The video game addiction rate is between eight percent and twelve percent worldwide based on research by several research groups and Douglas Gentile, PhD.[49, 50] The problem is, as a society in general, we are not educated about the long-term mental and health risks of video game addiction, nor are we taught what warning signs to watch for in our children, friends, spouses, and selves. Video games are sometimes free and available everywhere, and people are unaware of the one in ten who can and will become addicted to video games. Video game addicts can destroy their lives and the lives of the people they love. It's time our society understands this addiction, works to prevent it, and helps the one in ten who are addicted to video games.

Patria, a recovering video game addict who played World of Warcraft, states: "As a society we don't understand this [video game addiction] yet. I sure didn't when I picked up the game. I was in my fifties, old enough to know not to pick up another drug. But games were offered as fun, relaxing, and exciting, which is perfect for a fifty-something woman looking for something to do that doesn't

49 GETNILE ET AL. "PATHOLOGICAL VIDEO GAME USE AMONG YOUTH: A TWO-YEAR LONGITUDINAL STUDY." PEDIATRICS, 2011, 127, E319-329.
50 GENTILE D. "COMPUTER AND VIDEO GAME "ADDICTION." HTTP:// DRDOUGLAS.ORG/ISSUE01.HTML. ACCESSED SEPTEMBER 5, 2011.

*require a lot of activity. But, guess what? I got
addicted. Surprise! Surprise! Now that I am aware,
I cringe at people giving their kids games, and I
cringe at all the advertisements for games."*

As a physician, I see patients who develop dry eyes because they resist blinking when playing video games. Video game addiction is so strong a behavioral addiction that the addict resists blinking, eating, using the restroom, and taking care of personal hygiene; it sometimes leads to death due to poor nutrition and associated health problems. One of my colleagues shared with me that her eight-year-old child does the "potty wiggle" while playing video games, fighting the urge to use the toilet.

Dr. Eric Hollander at the Mt. Sinai School of Medicine, states that Internet and video game addiction can be associated with physical symptoms and withdrawals. Dr. Hollander sometimes prescribes antidepressants, mood stabilizers like Lithium, and opiate blockers like Naltrexone for people suffering from video game addiction.[51] Another study published in the *Journal of the American Academy of Pediatrics* found that video game addiction,

---

51 CBS SEGMENT GAMING ADDICTION [VIDEO]. YOUTUBE. 2007. HTTP://WWW.YOUTUBE.COM/WATCH?V=YBASIRI2GFU ACCESSED SEPTEMBER 5, 2011.

similar to other addictive behaviors, can last for years.[52] Some people blame video game addiction on the gamer being depressed or having social anxiety. However, the study in the *Journal of the American Academy of Pediatrics* showed that video game addiction can exist completely independent of these types of disorders. Another study showed that people who are craving Internet games exhibit changes in the prefrontal cortex, where addictive behaviors are controlled.[53] Video game addiction is becoming a worldwide crisis.

---

52 GENTILE ET AL. "PATHOLOGICAL VIDEO GAME USE AMONG YOUTHS: A TWO-YEAR LONGITUDINAL STUDY." PEDIATRICS. 2011 FEB;127(2):E319-29. EPUB 2011 JAN 17.
53 HAN ET AL. "CHANGES IN CUE-INDUCED, PREFRONTAL CORTEX ACTIVITY WITH VIDEO GAME PLAY." CYBERPSYCHOL BEHAV SOC NETW. 2010 DEC; 13(6). EPUB 2010 MAY 11.

Chapter 14: Breaking the Addiction

Before the person addicted to video games can start the journey to healing, the signs of addiction must be recognized. In this chapter, you can substitute the term "video games" with the words "Internet" or "social media websites," too.

"Video game addiction" and "Internet addiction" are not yet official medical diagnoses with standardized criteria. The following signs and symptoms of video game addiction are based on my experiences as a video game addict, my Interviews with therapists who work with video game addicts, and discussions with other video game addicts. According to the *On-Line Gamers Anonymous* website (http://www.olganon.org/), there are several signs of video game addiction:

Unable to estimate time spent gaming.

Unable to control gaming for an extended period of time.

Sense of euphoria while playing.

Hooked on Games

Craving more game time.

Neglecting family and friends.

Restless, irritable, or discontented when not gaming.

Lying about the amount of time gaming.

Experiencing problems with school or job performance.

Feeling guilt, shame, anxiety, or
depression as a result of gaming.

Change in sleep patterns.

Health issues such as carpal tunnel syndrome, eye-strain, weight change, backache, etc.

Denying, minimizing, and rationalizing the bad consequences of gaming.

Withdrawing from and neglecting real-life hobbies.

Obsession about acting out sexual
fantasies through the Internet.

Creation of an enhanced persona to find cyber-love

or cyber-sex.

Eating an increasing number of meals at the computer while gaming.

Increased time surfing game-related websites.

Constant conversation about the video game with uninterested friends or family.

Continued attempts to convince friends and family members to play.

Purchasing in-game items with real-life money.

Feeling the need to stand up for other gamers.

Continually bringing up life achievements to rationalize playing games for hours each day, e.g. "I provide for the family, and therefore I deserve to play as much as I like."

Other signs of video game addiction come from the Iowa State University study by Douglas Gentile, PhD.[54] The research by Dr. Gentile implies that a child is pathologically addicted to video gaming if he or she answers

54 GENTILE, D. "PATHOLOGICAL VIDEO-GAME USE AMONG YOUTH AGES 8 TO 18." PSYCHOL SCI. 2009 JUN; 20(6): 785.

"yes" to six or more of these questions. The following questions are based on diagnostic criteria for addictive gambling behavior:

Have you been spending an increasing amount of time playing video games, learning about video game playing, or planning the next opportunity to play?

Do you need to spend more time and money on video games in order to feel the same amount of excitement as you do with other activities in your life?

Have you tried to play video games for shorter durations of time without success?

Do you become restless or irritable when you attempt to cut down or stop playing video games?

Have you played video games as a way to escape problems or negative feelings?

Have you lied to family or friends about how much you play video games?

Have you ever stolen a video game from a store or a friend, or stolen money to buy a video game?

Do you sometimes skip household chores in order to play more video games?

Do you sometimes skip homework or work in order to play more video games?

Have you ever done poorly on a school assignment, test, or work assignment because you have spent so much time playing video games?

Have you ever needed friends or family to give you extra money because you've spent too much of your own money on video games, software, or game Internet fees?

SIGNS OF WITHDRAWAL FROM VIDEO GAMES

The *On-Line Gamers Anonymous* website also points out that some withdrawal symptoms that gamers can experience are very real and can be very extreme. I have experienced most of these symptoms in the height of my addiction to video games. These can include:

Anger and verbal abuse.

Feelings of emptiness, depression, or relief.

Disruption of sleep.

Fantasies and dreams about gaming.

The urge to go back to gaming and to attempt to control the time played.

Obsessing about the game for long periods of time.

Rampant, uncontrolled mood swings.

Excessive crying, fear, irritability, or restlessness.

Sadness, loneliness, or boredom.

Inability to find new activities or interests.

Lack of motivation or direction.

Excessive amounts of time spent sleeping.

Difficulty facing obligations.

Feeling as though returning to gaming will solve problems.

Physical symptoms such as nausea, allergies, colds, hemorrhoids, dry eyes, urinary incontinence, and constipation.

Restless, unfulfilling, and taunting dreams.

If you think someone you love is addicted to video games or the Internet, I've outlined some things you can do to help remove the stimulus of addictive behavior. These suggestions were derived from my personal experiences and from the discussions and advice found on the *On-Line Gamers Anonymous* website.

If the person lives in your home, you set the ground rules. Don't forget that. The worst thing you can do is to facilitate and enable the addictive behavior.

Cancel Internet access. If they can't access the Internet, they can't play. This sounds simple, but having open access to the Internet introduces an enormous digital buffet of video games. Many games are free on the Internet because revenues are generated from advertising. The gamer does not need money to start playing. Video game addicts lose the ability to self-moderate. They cannot have open access to the Internet.

Remove the computer from the person's room. Consider placing the computer in a public area of the home so that you can monitor the amount of game playing that is occurring. All computers should be locked down with passwords that the video game addict does not know.

Give the person a higher purpose. Help him or her focus on other hobbies of interest and to try church or small groups in order to make a connection with God and people who will offer support.

Do not enable gamers in any way. Don't pay for the Internet bill. Don't pay for monthly game subscriptions. Don't call in sick for them. Don't bring food to the computer while they're gaming. Don't do their laundry or clean their room.

If you suspect that there is depression or any other mental illness present, seek professional medical help immediately. As illustrated in previous chapters, gaming and suicide have been linked. If you suspect the person has any suicidal thoughts, seek help quickly.

Be aware of the withdrawal symptoms, and be mindful that professional medical help may be needed.

For a child, when possible, address the gaming addiction before sending them away to college. Visit where they will be living. Do they have access to the Internet 24/7? It is common for gaming addicts to spiral quickly out of control after leaving their parents' home because of the sudden freedom and inability to regulate their game-play, and some addicted college students lose their scholarships or even flunk out of school.

If the person is in his or her own living environment and financially independent, print out articles on gaming addiction, give them a copy of this book, or provide a link to the *On-Line Gamers Anonymous* website. However, keep in mind that these efforts are futile until the gamer admits to having a problem and is willing to accept help. You can lead a horse to water, but you cannot make the horse drink.

Be kind and understanding. These games were designed to be enticing and addictive. If the game isn't addictive, it doesn't make money.

Remember that he or she is not a bad person. Addiction of this nature is an illness and sympathy is important.

Play video games as a family so that it is a social or a team event, but place time limits on the duration.

The best way to fight video game addiction is prevention. We must be educated about the dangers of excessive video game play. Allowing children to play at young ages and for long periods of time reinforces addictive behaviors. As a society, we must stop using video games and the Internet as digital pacifiers; we need to educate children and adults about the dangers of video game addiction and promote responsible use.

I encourage those who are addicted to video games to seek professional help. Medications, such as anti-depressants, Lithium, and Naltrexone, can be used under the supervision of a physician to help with the withdrawal, depression, anxiety, and other symptoms associated with video game addiction.[55, 56] Psychotherapy is useful for identifying the root causes from which the video game addict may be suffering. Identifying root causes facilitates addressing the issues that led to the addictive behavior. For video game addicts who are deep in their addiction, professional intervention will be necessary and strongly advised.

The video game addict must address the root causes leading to the behavioral addiction. Otherwise, relapse will occur. Over the years of training and working with my church in the marriage mentor program and as a Celebrate Recovery leader, I have found that the root causes of addictions are profound personal hurts, habits, and hang-ups. We all have varying degrees of emotional baggage; some we can let go but others we hold onto. The ones we hold onto will affect us until we identify and address them. For instance, if a person was abused as a child and unable to develop self-confidence in real

55 HAN ET AL. "BUPROPION SUSTAINED RELEASE TREATMENT DECREASES CRAVING FOR VIDEO GAMES AND CUE-INDUCED BRAIN ACTIVITY IN PATIENTS WITH INTERNET VIDEO GAME ADDICTION." EXP CLIN PSYCHOPHARMACOL. 2010 AUG; 18(4): 297-304.
56 CBS SEGMENT GAMING ADDICTION [VIDEO]. YOUTUBE. 2007. HTTP://WWW.YOUTUBE.COM/WATCH?V=YBASIRI2GFU ACCESSED SEPTEMBER 5, 2011.

life, then the person may turn to video games where he has control and power. But unless the issue of abuse is addressed, the video game addict will relapse and continue to turn to the digital world for escape. The addict may trade one addiction for another, turning to drugs, alcohol, food, or other harmful addictive behaviors.

I encourage addicts to try the options offered by the secular world if God is not a part of their life and they're not yet willing to consider God as an option. If the secular world alone does not succeed in helping with the video game addiction or addictive behavior, then please read this entire chapter with an open mind and heart and allow God to help. God will heal past hurts, habits, and hang-ups associated with the root causes of video game addiction and other behavioral addictions.

After a decade of playing video games forty to fifty hours a week and relapsing again and again, the only thing that worked for me was to become strong in mind, body, and spirit. If one component was weak, the other two consumed me. If my mind was uneducated, then I was a fool. If my body was weak, then I suffered from health problems. If my spirit was weak, then I was a bully with emotional baggage. Now I strengthen my mind by fulfilling my thirst for knowledge and continually learning new things. I keep my body disease-free by eating healthy and exercising. The only thing I have discovered to fill my spirit is humbly submitting to God, following Jesus, and pursuing His plan for me.

My road to recovery was wholly dependent on my finding God. When I was an atheist or an agnostic, I spent my time searching for love and purpose on my own, through things that made me feel good; and that turned into a full-fledged addiction to video games for over nine years of my life. For others, their addiction can be gambling, smoking, weight loss, eating, alcohol, or drugs. My addiction was to video games, which facilitated my escape into a digital fantasy world. But I felt no peace trying to fulfill the deep longing inside me for acceptance and true, complete love. I believed I had the power within me to fix and control my addiction. I was wrong.

Eventually, God helped me to see my value and purpose. I read a book for my first Bible study, *The Purpose Driven Life* by Rick Warren, and through the words in this book, God helped me to find my passion, to discover my dreams, to realize His love, and to unlock the blueprint He had for my life. After this realization, I eventually stopped playing video games and started focusing my time on God-honoring activities. I began pouring myself into my family—by expressing my love better towards my wife, helping to teach my children, and starting to build legacies to serve others. I played the game of real life, using the Bible as my rules of engagement. It was almost instantaneous: as soon as I focused my heart on God instead of on video games, I was able to begin destroying my old self and allow God to reveal my true soul, rebuilding what I had so selfishly destroyed for years. I found complete acceptance and safety in the arms of God. He provided me with everything I sought as a human being that I couldn't find for myself. Soon, I realized that I didn't have to turn to addiction to numb my mind, to escape, or to get through the day. Once I found my purpose—a higher calling through God as my higher power—my life began to be blessed daily.

Now that the signs and symptoms of video game addiction and withdrawal are laid out, finding a way to address the problem and to promote healing is imperative. In addition to understanding my God-given purpose in life, I have found support in attending Celebrate Recovery meetings, which are focused on addressing all hurts, habits, and hang-ups that affect people and cause them to return to their addictive natures. Celebrate Recovery is a program designed by Pastor John Baker and Pastor Rick Warren at Saddleback Church.[57] There are thousands of Celebrate Recovery programs across the country, and the program is highly successful. I've found that I'm free to walk in the purpose I have in God and that it's easy to rise to His expectations. In God, I have the

---

57 CELEBRATE RECOVERY WEBSITE. HTTP://WWW. CELEBRATERECOVERY.COM/. ACCESSED SEPTEMBER 4, 2011.

power to fight the addiction and the power to pursue my dreams. Not only do I have the power to do this, but I can do it with fervor because of the calling He gives me.

The twelve steps in the Celebrate Recovery program have been key in fighting and winning the battle over addictions. I encourage video game and Internet addicts to seek a local Celebrate Recovery program to help them with their recovery. Fighting addictions is difficult without face-to-face sponsors, accountability partners, and local support. Based on the Alcoholics Anonymous twelve-step program, the success of Celebrate Recovery is attributable to being centered on Jesus Christ, and the steps are biblically founded.

Since Celebrate Recovery began, over 10,000 people at Saddleback have completed the program and found victory over their hurts, habits, and hang-ups through Christ's power. Celebrate Recovery has launched in over 17,000 churches and 700,000 people have completed the program. Celebrate Recovery is a program for alcoholics, co-dependents, people with eating disorders, those struggling with sexual addictions, those in need of anger management, those dealing with past or current physical or sexual abuse issues, those in need of financial recovery, and many more groups. In short, anyone dealing with any kind of hurt, habit, or hang-up can find help through the Celebrate Recovery program.

CELEBRATE RECOVERY'S TWELVE STEPS

I have applied these twelve steps to my life as it pertains to my video game addiction. I hope and pray that the breakdown of these steps will help other video game addicts address their own struggle with their addiction.

1) We admitted we were powerless over our addictions and compulsive behaviors, and that our lives have become unmanageable. (Romans 7:18 NIV—I know that nothing good lives in me, that is, in my sinful nature. For I have the desire to do what is good, but I cannot carry it out.)

These compulsive and addictive behaviors are so strong that without admitting that we are powerless over them, we will ultimately let technology control us. Jesus taught that a person could only serve one of two masters. If a person serves one then the person has to shun the other. For some of us, playing video games in moderation is simply not possible. Games can be great; there are some that help people with hand-eye coordination and there are some that facilitate learning. There are people who can play in moderation, simply as entertainment. But for millions of addicts, the need to play will become a true addiction, and we must keep in mind that on our own we are weak and will always be powerless over video game addiction. We won't allow technology to be a master over us and must avoid worshiping technology and video games as false idols.

2) We came to believe that a Power greater than ourselves could restore us to sanity. (Philippians 2:13 NIV—For it is God who is at work in you to will and to act according to His good purpose.)

As human beings, we are weak. We are susceptible to sickness, injury, temptation, and death. But when we know there is a power greater than ourselves, we possess great comfort and strength to live lives of hope with confidence. We have the ability to move forward. The Higher Power has to be God. When people choose higher powers that have no true power, relapse is inevitable. Even other people cannot be the higher power. People are imperfect; they will fail from time to time, and they may hurt us. God is always perfect; He is loving, and good. He is the Higher Power that is able to restore our sanity.

3) We made a decision to turn our will and our lives over to the care of God. (Romans 12:1 NIV—Therefore, I urge you, brothers, in view of God's mercy, to offer your bodies as living sacrifices, holy and pleasing to God—this is your spiritual act of worship.)

We are not in control of our lives. If we realize our higher purpose and we trust God, when trials come our way we won't start moaning and complaining. Instead, we will look at those trials as opportunities to be molded, to be taught, to be challenged and to rise up and become who we've been created to be—in God's eyes, not man's eyes. The challenges we face will help us to become better than we were yesterday. For example, a lump of coal without heat or pressure will only be a lump of coal. But with the right combination of heat and pressure, a lump of coal has the potential to be transformed into a beautiful diamond. The heat and pressure that we experience in our own lives and how we use them are the forces molding us into better people. We can face our hardships head-on knowing that, by trusting God, something good will come out of it.

4) We made a searching and fearless moral inventory of ourselves. (Lamentations 3:40 NIV—Let us examine our ways and test them, and let us return to the Lord.)

The key to this step is that we have to take continual inventory of ourselves to learn where we came from and why we have these addictive natures. For me, I look to my childhood and can pinpoint hurts, insecurities, yearning for love, and other needs that weren't being met. Without honestly examining myself and acknowledging issues that have led up to my addictions, I was unable to move forward and win the battle over excessive gaming.

5) We admitted to God, ourselves, and to another human being the exact nature of our wrongs. (James 5:16 NIV—Therefore, confess your sins to each other, and pray for each other, so that you may be healed.)

We must admit that we have done wrong and that our video game addiction has hurt other people. If we can't admit this, we simply can't heal. This requires strength and humility to admit to others that we have done wrong and hurt them. But, by embracing this step, we are free to move forward with humility.

6) We were entirely ready to have God remove all these defects of character. (James 4:10 NIV—Humble yourselves before the Lord, and he will lift you up.)

Once you're ready for God to help remove the defects of your character, He will. You will feel love, confidence, and security. You will gain a healthy ego and be a better leader who can help not only yourself but others around you. Knowing God's love, I know who I am in God's eyes and do not depend on the opinions of others for my self-confidence and ego. This is counter-intuitive, but by leaning on God and depending on Him, we discover strength, confidence, and incredible freedom.

7) We humbly asked Him to remove all our shortcomings. (1 John 1:9 NIV—If we confess our sins, he is faithful and just and will forgive us our sins and purify us from all unrighteousness.)

Being humble is the key to eliminating our own selfish desires and walking in the light that God has given us. We must confess that we are broken individuals and must daily ask God to heal us and help us face our short-comings head on. When we are humble, God lifts us up. God is constant and never changes. He is the source of our ego, strength, and freedom.

8) We made a list of all persons we had harmed and became willing to make amends to them all. (Luke 6:31 NIV—Do to others as you would have them do to you.)

I harmed my wife, my children, my extended fami-ly, my friends, and even those in my professional cir-cles. As difficult as this step initially was, once I did it I felt freedom and peace. The weight of my addic-tion was lifted off of me, and I was able to move for-ward and take steps toward recovery and growth.

9) We made direct amends to such people whenever possible, except when to do so would injure them or others. (Matthew 5:23-24 NIV—Therefore, if you are offering your gift at the altar and there remember that your brother has something against you, leave your gift there in front of the altar. First go and be reconciled to your brother; then come and offer your gift.)

This is where discretion is sometimes needed; you should not confront a person if you know it is going to harm them. It may be helpful to have a face-to-face sponsor through the Celebrate Recovery program who can help walk you through this process.

10) We continued to take personal inventory and when we were wrong promptly admitted it. (1 Corinthians 10:12 NIV—So, if you think you are standing firm, be careful that you don't fall!)

Continually evaluate yourself. Make certain you're still emotionally healthy. Examine your heart. Make sure that the hurts, habits, and hang-ups that initially drew you to video game addiction are dealt with. If you're not moving forward or are considering relapse, it is essential that you take this seriously. Admit to someone about the battle that is waging within you, and seek help to fight it. You must also be honest with yourself. Addicts are notorious liars.

11) We sought through prayer and meditation to improve our conscious contact with God, praying only for knowledge of His will for us and power to carry that out. (Colossians 3:16a NIV—Let the word of Christ dwell in you richly.)

Attend church and Bible studies. Attend Celebrate Recovery meetings. The more you know about God and what He has to say, the more success you'll experience in life—in your relationships, your education, your work, your physical health, your business, and your goals. Immerse yourself in God's word and then apply it to your life. My life is a testimony of what God restored. He saved my marriage and my career. He has blessed me.

12) Having had a spiritual experience as a result of these steps, we try to carry this message to others and practice these principles in all our affairs. (Galatians 6:1 NIV—Brothers, if someone is caught in a sin, you who are spiritual should restore him gently. But watch yourself or you also may be tempted.)

As addicts, we will always be susceptible to relapse. To this day, I cannot play any MMORPG, turn based, role-playing or real-time-strategy video games. I cannot play video games in moderation. I have acknowledged that I will always be an addict, and I have to avoid anything that might trigger a reversion back to my addiction. But knowing that I have been healed through God, I also understand that I must help others who are struggling with this type of addiction. Sharing my knowledge and my experience with others through mentorship is a way to remind me of my own weaknesses. It also helps to remind me of the truth of what it takes to heal, and it reminds me to focus myself on God and the blessings He has given me, despite my failures and shortcomings. God is awesome.

Let's again consider Steve who faced video game addiction as a teenager. His parents realized that he was showing the signs of addiction and that they had to set new rules. They cut his playing time down to the weekends only. When that didn't work, Steve's parents limited him to only an hour on the weekend. That also didn't work, so they changed the playing time to only on holidays. Steve anticipated and yearned for his game time, as if he was waiting for his next "fix." He was yearning for it intensely. Finally, his parents evaluated the situation as a whole, recognized that there was nothing good coming out of it, and decided to completely remove all games from the home. Steve went through a period of withdrawal. He was sad, angry, and even wished his mother's death because she was so adamant about the gaming coming to an end.

Within six months of removing and selling all of his games, Steve's grade point average went up from a 3.0 to a 4.0. He became the most valuable player on his soccer team. As an incoming freshman in high school, he won the soccer-juggling contest. He poured himself into learning web design and built websites. He began focusing on the youth group at church and fostering real-life friendships. He focused more on God-honoring activities. His parents had helped direct Steve's attention to activities that were positive. Another rule Steve's parents made was that all video games played in the house must be played as a family. For example, they have a Wii and they must all play interactive games together as a family. Video games are played as a family event with strict time limits. Not allowing the video game addict to be isolated in a video game or Internet activity is critical to curtailing the behavioral addiction.

Addicts will trade one addiction for another. Social media and texting can be huge problems but can be effective ways of communicating when used properly. We live in a digital age. We cannot isolate ourselves completely from technology. Educating ourselves on responsible use is essential. Like video game addiction, however, if one cannot use it in moderation, then abstinence is the solution. For Steve, Facebook time is limited to less than thirty minutes per day on the weekends. This limitation allows Steve to communicate with friends without exhibiting signs of obsession or addiction. All computers are password-protected, and Steve must ask permission to use the computer located in the kitchen. Steve wanted a cell phone for communication purposes. His parents limited the texting to fifty texts per week. Each additional text is twenty-five cents owed to his parents. With the texting rule in place, Steve limits his texting. Finally, Steve understands the harm associated with video game addiction; he is educated to make good decisions. He knows that his future depends on it.

Conclusion: Generation Vidiot

In Disney's hit movie *Wall-E,* humans have destroyed the earth, and all of humanity had been forced to live in space. The humans are digitally plugged in, and are transported around space in all sorts of unique space-craft, relying solely on computer-controlled, automated systems that regulate their environments. Because the humans become dependent on these automated systems, they begin experiencing morbid obesity and bone loss. They become mindless individuals in their virtual reality. *USA Today* writer Claudia Puig described the humans in *Wall-E* this way: "The descendants of those who populated Earth have become massive, flabby beings with tiny, almost-vestigial limbs. They spend their days in moving recliners equipped with screens, in their own virtual worlds, avoiding human contact."[58]

Are we creating generations of "vidiots" as well? As our society becomes more and more plugged in, are we going to see a loss of talent and innovation? Are we clouding the minds of our youth?

---

58 PUIG, CLAUDIA. "REVIEW: WALL-E PLUGS INTO HUMAN EMOTION." USA TODAY. JUNE 27, 2008. HTTP://WWW.USATODAY.COM/LIFE/ MOVIES/REVIEWS/2008-06-25-WALL-E_N.HTM. ACCESSED SEPTEMBER 12, 2011.

I was invited to speak to 100 students at a local high school about the signs and dangers of video game addiction. The teacher asked the class to anonymously fill out the video game addiction survey published by Dr. Gentile.[59] One in ten students in the class exhibited behaviors consistent with video game addiction, and more than half of the class indicated that they knew others who might have a problem with excessive video game playing. Game designers have known about the role of dopamine in designing "addicting games". In a *New York Times* article on the addictive nature of technology, the following was noted about the addictive nature of on-line games, "Eric Schiermeyer, a co-founder of Zynga, an online game company and maker of huge hits like *Farm-Ville*, has said he has helped addict millions of people to dopamine, a neurochemical that has been shown to be released by pleasurable activities, including video game playing, but also is understood to play a major role in the cycle of addiction."[60]

Before my presentation, the students did not know about video game addiction. But, after being educated about the dangers of video game addiction, the students

59 GENTILE, D. "PATHOLOGICAL VIDEO-GAME USE AMONG YOUTH AGES 8 TO 18." PSYCHOL SCI. 2009 JUN; 20(6): 785.
60 RITCHEL, M. "SILICON VALLEY SAYS STEP AWAY FROM THE DEVICE". THE NEW YORK TIMES. JULY 23, 2012. HTTP://WWW.NYTIMES. COM/2012/07/24/TECHNOLOGY/SILICON-VALLEY-WORRIES-ABOUT-ADDICTION-TO-DEVICES.HTML?_R=1&ADXNNL=1&REF=GENERAL &SRC=ME&ADXNNLX=1343300437-DESVHGXDNY5QJKLJVE%2FQHA. ACCESSED JULY 25, 2012.

felt informed, enlightened, and better equipped to make decisions about video games and Internet use. For the kids who may possibly have a problem with excessive use of video games, I encouraged them to discuss the issue with their parents and to consider seeking help.

People are trading one addiction for another. If it's not video games, it might be YouTube, Facebook, or texting on their cell phones. If it's not video games, it might be alcohol, sex, drugs, or food. People, and particularly our youth, are completely plugged in. For example, with texting, kids are asking and talking about things that are inappropriate and that they might not be comfortable talking about face to face, especially things of a sexual nature. But when they get a text back in response, it breaks the barriers of caution and brings a sense of euphoria, similar to a high when playing a video game. Texting people in rapid-fire succession while getting immediate responses in return provides feelings of acceptance and excitement. People have turned to technology to communicate and have forgotten how to talk to each other. Kids today are losing the ability to interact with people. They're not being properly socialized.

We encourage families and parents to wake up and take action to avoid raising a generation of vidiots who live in seclusion, separated from the rest of the world; they need to teach kids and young adults about the responsible use of technology. It's clear that using technology and video games as digital pacifiers is potentially harmful, both mentally and physically. Being interested, active, and involved in the lives of our kids, teenagers, and spouses is vital to keeping them on the right path, away from addiction. Spending real, face-to-face time communicating and enjoying the company of loved ones teach us to be more human, too.

For young people who are prone to addiction, this parental involvement in their lives might be the very thing that helps them channel their energy into productive and fulfilling pursuits. Oftentimes, an addictive personality towards video games and technology is the sign of intelligence and passion in a person. Given the chance, they might achieve great things. If they can turn the tables and become a master of technology rather than a slave to it, the sky's the limit.

Consider the Internet success story of www.fitocracy.com, a website founded by a former video game addict, Richard Talens. Richard grew up playing video games. He was from foreign-born parents living in the Marshall Islands, a third world country. His extremely addictive personality led him to easily get into games and lose track of time when he was gaming. He obsessed over the games. Even before his teen years he could easily play for twelve hours at one sitting. His obsession with video games led him to become anti-social, adopting a bad diet and experiencing significant weight gain. Richard weighed about 170 pounds by the time he was twelve years old. He moved to the United States and did not have many friends; so he found purpose and a social life in playing MMORPGs. By the time he was sixteen years old, he weighed about 230 pounds and was fully addicted to *EverQuest*. One summer, he played nonstop from waking up until bedtime, taking breaks only to eat. One day, Richard realized he was physically ill because of his own behavior. He was slowly killing himself. He immediately gave away all of his virtual *EverQuest* possessions, quit playing, and started researching nutrition and diets.

Richard focused his gaming mentality and drive into fitness and became a body builder, always trying to outdo himself. Instead of working to get to the next level in a game, he channeled that same energy into real life "level-ups." By the time he was twenty years old, he had competed and placed in his first body-building contest—a far cry from where he had been three years previous. The gaming mentality allowed him to make a rapid transformation for the better in his life. He learned to hone in on different skills, and he quit his job to start www.fitocracy.com in October 2010, and eight months later, his website had over 100,000 users with another 100,000 on the waiting list. Richard attributed his success in business to the same gaming mentality he always had—being able to analyze a situation quickly, figure out how to get better, and obsessively reach that goal.

Similarly, I have learned to focus the energy and drive I had when gaming into entrepreneurship and God-honoring activities. When I stopped playing, I focused on building up my wife and kids. I worked on applying biblical principals to my daily life. After I quit gaming and gained an extra forty hours of "free time" per week, I started a publishing company, www.medrounds.org, and founded Eye Associates of Southern California (www.eye-socal.com), a hybrid medical clinic serving both the insured and uninsured. With my free time away from gaming, I also learned web design, search engine optimization and management, and Internet marketing. I developed a system for Verified Reviews® through Credential Protection (www.credentialprotection.com) to protect doctors' online reputations and patients' rights to have accurate information about their doctors. Credential Protection was selected as one of the top 10-startup companies out of more than 110 companies at Vator Splash LA 2012. I am part of the ministry team at Rancho Community Church, serving as a Celebrate Recovery 12-Step leader for people suffering from gaming, gambling, and Internet addictions.

None of these endeavors would have been possible if I had remained addicted to the digital world. Instead of building a legacy with my family, I would be creating guilds online. Rather than developing relationships with the other men at the Men's Group at church on Saturday morning, I would have been leveling my toons in a MMORPG. Instead of creating jobs with new businesses, I would be hooked on games. Most importantly, instead of serving others in the community and developing a relationship with God, I would still be lost in a digital world and consumed physically, emotionally, and spiritually by video games.

The lure of the digital world is a bright and shining trap. It pretends to offer everything the human being craves, and once the hurting, addictive personality catches a glimpse of the bait, they're ensnared. Like a moth, grazing a spider's web with his wing, just that one touch is enough. By the time the moth realizes he's trapped, it's too late. The spider is upon him. The moth's attempts to escape are futile, and the spider injects the deadly venom. Likewise, the video game addict often doesn't wake up to the fact that their life is being destroyed until it is already too late. I'm thankful every day that I was given a chance to struggle free just before the venom of addiction wreaked irreparable havoc in my life. I pray this book provides that chance of escape for others who are addicted like I was.

If we don't educate ourselves and our family members

about the responsible use of games, technology, and the Internet, we're exposing our children, families, and loved ones to a potentially vicious cycle of video game and Internet addiction. Moderation is key to living a rewarding and happy life. I am a passionate and intense individual who enjoys diving into tasks with full devotion. Thus, it's difficult for me to live in moderation, and I continually have to remind myself (with the help of my wife) to take a deep breath and to take it easy.

If playing video games in moderation is easy for you, then it's unlikely you'll be hooked on games. If not, making the decision to unplug completely and to stop playing must happen, because too much of anything will be harmful to your health. Remember, even water in excess can be deadly.

Some of you who are reading this book may not believe that video games are addictive and may not agree that video game addiction is a real illness. Some of you may not think it can happen to you or to your loved ones. Yet the stories in this book are true. Let my story be a lesson to you. Video game addiction almost destroyed my marriage, my family, and my medical career. It almost took my life.

B r e a k i n g   F r e e

For God so loved the world that he gave his one and only Son, that whoever believes in him shall not perish but have eternal life. – John 3:16, New International Version

If you have not accepted Jesus as your Lord and Savior, then I invite you to do so. Allow God to heal you and to strengthen your mind, body and spirit. I encourage you to seek a Celebrate Recovery program and work through the 12-Steps with God as your Higher Power.

Pray the following out loud: "Dear Lord, I confess my sins to you. Please forgive me of my sins and addictions. I invite you, Jesus, into my life. As my Lord and Savior, please guide me and strengthen my mind, body, and spirit so I will be free of my hurts, habits, and hang-ups. In Jesus' Name, AMEN!"

Therefore, if anyone is in Christ, he is a new creation; the old has gone, the new has come! – 2 Corinthians 5:17, New International Version

About the Author

Dr. Doan practices comprehensive ophthalmology and eye pathology and is board certified by the American Board of Ophthalmology. Dr. Doan treats a broad range of eye disorders including eye cancers and tumors. Born in Saigon, Vietnam and raised in Oregon, he earned a Bachelor of Arts degree in Biology from Reed College. He completed his MD and PhD degrees at The Johns Hopkins University School of Medicine. Dr. Doan completed both an Internal Medicine Internship and General Clinical and Surgical Ophthalmology residency at the University of Iowa. After his ophthalmology training, he completed his fellowship in eye pathology at the Jules Stein Eye Institute at the University of California, Los Angeles. Dr. Doan volunteers as a clinical provider at the Temecula-Murrieta Rescue Mission, serving patients with the help of the team at Eye Associates of Southern California. He is an Assistant Professor of Surgery at Loma Linda University. Dr. Doan teaches medical students and residents, is published in peer-reviewed academic journals, is managing editor for the *Journal of Academic Ophthalmology*, and speaks at national meetings. Dr. Doan has served as Chair for the Young Ophthalmologist committee, Ophthalmic News & Education Network

Deputy Editor-in-Chief, and an OPHTHPAC/Congressional Advocacy Committee member for the American Academy of Ophthalmology. In addition, Dr. Doan has served on the Risk Management Committee for the Ophthalmic Mutual Insurance Company.

After being freed from his addiction to video games and living by biblical principals, Dr. Doan launched several companies, including a publishing company, www.medrounds.org, www.credentialprotection.com, www.eye-socal.com, and www.vireomd.com to serve the medical community and patients. Dr. Doan is working on his second book with author Marie Hunt, The *Biggest 24: Harnessing Your Full Potential In the Digital Age* (www.biggest24.com). When not pursuing his career interests, Dr. Doan enjoys spending time with family and serving at Rancho Community Church as a Celebrate Recovery 12-Step Leader for Gaming and Internet Addictions.

Appendix: Resources

There are several organizations, therapists, websites, and books related to video gaming and technology addiction as a whole. Many of these offer beneficial resources, counsel, and information that can help you or a loved one to overcome the addiction battle. While these resources are not a replacement for a recovery group or an in-person counseling meeting, we hope the information below will help serve as an additional support network. We offer these resources for your reference, but we do not have experience with every organization or resource listed. Additional information is found on our website at: www.hooked-on-games.com

Organizations and Websites

American Psychological Association
750 First St. NE
Washington, DC 20002
(800) 374-2721
www.apa.org

The American Psychological Association (APA) is a scientific and professional organization that represents psychology in the United States. It is the largest association of psychologists worldwide with more than 154,000 members. The site provides a variety of journals, articles, books, reports, and more.

Celebrate Recovery
www.celebraterecovery.com

Celebrate Recovery is a Christ-centered recovery program for people with addictive behaviors. The 12-step program helps people with hurts, habits, and hang-ups. This recovery program has been launched in over 17,000 churches and has over 700,000 graduates.

The Center for Successful Parenting
www.sosparents.org

This site provides parents with the opportunity to understand the effects on children who view video violence. It has links to new scientific studies on the topic, research citations, tips for parents, news updates, and more.

Center on Media and Child Health
300 Longwood Ave.
Boston, MA 02115
(617) 355-2000
www.cmch.tv

The vision of this organization is to educate and empower

children and those who care for them by teaching them to create and consume media in ways that optimize children's health and development. The website offers information on understanding the effects of media on the physical, mental, and social health of children. There are resources for parents, teachers, and a complete database where individuals can ask questions about media and health.

Common Sense Media
650 Townsend St., Suite 375
San Francisco, CA 94103
(415) 863-0600
www.commonsensemedia.org

This non-profit organization offers trustworthy advice, articles, and resources in an independent, non-partisan forum for families and kids. There are free educator resources, tips on everything digital including reviews of games and other digital sources, and age-specific content for kids.

Entertainment Software Association
575 7th St. NW, Suite 300
Washington, DC 20004
www.theesa.com

The Entertainment Software Association is "exclusively dedicated to serving the business and public affairs needs of companies that publish computer and video games for video game consoles, personal computers, and the Internet." The site includes facts about the video game industry, public policy information, articles, and news releases.

Entertainment Software Rating Board
317 Madison Ave., 22nd floor
New York, NY 10173
www.esrb.org

The Entertainment Software Rating Board "assigns computer and video game content ratings, enforces industry-adopted advertising guidelines, and helps ensure responsible online privacy practices for the interactive entertainment software industry." The site helps consumers, especially parents to make informed decisions about computer and video games they're considering buying by assigning appropriate age and content ratings.

Fitocracy.com

Fitocracy is the game you play to improve your fitness. Play it to track your progress, compete against your friends, and get real results in your physical fitness. To play, just enter your fitness activities on the Track page every day. As you enter your activities into Fitocracy, you'll earn points. Over time, you'll earn enough points to get to the next level. Leveling up means you've been keeping up with your fitness. Fitocracy's mission is to make fitness a more fun, more addictive experience. Play Fitocracy to beat challenges, push your boundaries, and show your friends who's boss. Get addicted to your fitness.

My Addiction
(800) 401-3218 (24-hour treatment line)
www.myaddiction.com

This online recovery resource provides treatment information for a significant number of addictions. It offers information on support groups and treatment centers, has a blog, addiction-related video clips, and a glossary of addiction terms.

On-Line Gamers Anonymous
1300 Pennsylvania Ave. NW
Washington, DC 20004
(612) 245-1115
www.olganon.org

The mission of this organization is creating a "fellowship of people sharing their experience, strengths, and hopes to help each other recover and heal from the problems caused by excessive game playing." The site invites individuals to come together as a community to support one another, while offering information on 12-step programs, withdrawal symptoms, and recommended reading materials, updates on news stories, and more.

Books

Cyber Junkie: Escape the Gaming and Internet Trap
by Kevin Roberts
In Kevin Roberts' sober personal account of addiction, he reveals a modern society completely inundated with electronics. We are embroiled in stimuli from texting, chatting, social networking, casual gaming, and massive multi-user role-playing games that allow us to trade real life for highly stimulating virtual realities. For the majority of users, these stimuli provide a brief, entertaining diversion from the quotidian. But for some, they result in destroyed careers and relationships.

Fun Inc.: Why Gaming Will Dominate the Twenty-First Century by Tom Chatfield
Despite the recession, video games continue to break records—and command unprecedented amounts of media coverage. The United States is the world's biggest video games market and manufacturer, with a market now worth over $20 billion annually in software and hardware sales— more than quadruple its size in the mid 1990s. *World of Warcraft* now boasts over 11 million players worldwide and

over $1 billion per year in revenues. Gaming is flourishing as a career and a creative industry, as well. 254 U.S. colleges and universities in 37 states now offer courses and degrees in computer and video game design, programming, and art.

How to Help Children Addicted to Video Games
by Brent Conrad
Dr. Conrad is a clinical psychologist that specializes in treating adults, teens, and children that are addicted to video games. The book provides techniques and strategies that Dr. Conrad has used when working with parents and children struggling with the addiction.

Playstation Nation by Olivia and Kurt Bruner
This book, written by two parents who saw video game addiction tendencies developing in their son, shares personal stories of addiction to help other parents pinpoint the warning signs of addiction in their own children.

Unplugged: My Journey into the Dark World of Video Game Addiction by Ryan G. Van Cleave
WARNING: THIS VIDEO GAME MAY IMPAIR YOUR JUDGMENT. IT MAY CAUSE SLEEP DEPRIVATION, ALIENATION OF FRIENDS AND FAMILY, WEIGHT LOSS OR GAIN, NEGLECT OF YOUR BASIC NEEDS AS WELL AS THE NEEDS OF LOVED ONES AND/OR DEPENDENTS, AND DECREASED PERFORMANCE ON THE JOB. THE DISTINCTION

BETWEEN FANTASY AND REALITY MAY BECOME BLURRED. PLAY AT YOUR OWN RISK. NOT RESPONSIBLE FOR SUICIDE ATTEMPTS. No such warning was included on the latest and greatest release from the Warcraft series of massive multiplayer online role-playing games—*World of Warcraft*. So when Ryan Van Cleave—a college professor, husband, father, and one of the roughly 11 million Warcraft subscribers worldwide—found himself teetering on the edge of the Arlington Memorial Bridge, he had no one to blame but himself. He had neglected his wife and children and had jeopardized his livelihood, all for the rush of living a life of high adventure in a virtual world. For Ryan, the virtual world was a siren-song he couldn't ignore, no matter the cost. As is the case with most recovering addicts, Ryan eventually hit rock bottom and shares with you his ongoing battle to control his impulses to play, providing prescriptive advice and resources for those caught in the grip of this very real addiction.

Video Game Addiction Worldwide by James Miller
This book looks at video game addiction in both adults and children. Other topics include addiction social networking, pornography, and the health effects of technology addiction.

Therapy Centers

Illinois Institute for Addiction Recovery
5409 N. Knoxville Ave.
Peoria, IL 61614
(800) 522-3784
www.addictionrecov.org

This organization offers free, confidential assessments
over the phone, 24/7, where a professional counselor
can diagnose a variety of addiction disorders, including
video game addiction. They also offer further treatment
via phone appointments, as well as on-site classes and
workshops to provide education on addiction.

reSTART Internet Addiction Recovery Program
1001 290th Ave. SE
Fall City, WA 98604
(800) 682-6934
www.netaddictionrecovery.com

This is an intensive on-site treatment center for
problematic computer, video game, Internet, and cell
phone use. The program is individually tailored for
participants to help break the cycle of behavioral addiction
and dependency.

Counselors & Physicians

Jerald Block, MD
1314 NW Irving Street, Suite 508
Portland, OR 97209
(503) 241-4882

Jay Parker or Hilarie Cash, PhD
Internet/Computer Addiction Services
16307 NE 83rd St.
Redmond, WA 98052
(425) 802-9197 or (425) 861-5504

Ms. Joyce Dolberg Rowe, Counselor, Med, LMHC
The Door Is Open Counseling Center
92 Manomet Avenue
Hull, MA 02045
(781) 361-9914

Eric Hollander, MD
Department of Psychiatry and Behavioral Sciences
Montefiore Medical Center
3340 Bainbridge Ave., Room 304
Bronx, NY 10467
(718) 696-3035

David Greenfield, PhD
The Healing Center, LLC & The Center for Internet Behavior
12 North Main St., Suite 108
West Hartford, CT 06117
(860) 561-8727

Gary A. Grossman, PhD
1700 Coit Rd., Suite 110
Plano, Texas 75075
(972) 398-9452

Scott Peebles, M.A., MFCC, H.B.
Licensed Marriage, Family, and Child Counselor
Child, Teen, and Parenting Specialist
1151 Dove St., Suite 160
Newport Beach, CA 92660
(949) 833-1599

Karen Pierce, MD
Chicago's Children's Memorial Hospital
2300 Children's Plaza
Chicago, IL
(773) 880-4000
www.childrensmemorial.org

Kevin Roberts
Author of Cyber Junkie
Therepist and Interventionist
www.kevinjroberts.net

Claudia Vernon
Center for Individual and Family Therapy
5182 Katella, Suite 202
Los Alamitos, CA 90720
(866) 222-CIFT

Terry R. Waite
Sutter Center for Psychiatry
7700 Folsom Blvd.
Sacramento, CA 95826
(915) 386-3000
www.suttermedicalcenter.org/psychiatry/

Kenneth Woog, Psy.D.
3551 Camino Mira Costa, Suite K
San Clemente, CA 92672
949-422-4120
www.computergamingaddiction.com

Kimberly Young, PhD
eBehavior, LLC
P.O. Box 72
Bradford, PA 16701
(877) CYBER-DR
www.netaddiction.com

Made in the USA
San Bernardino, CA
12 November 2014